A guide

birds

of the
British Indian Ocean Territory

by Peter Carr

Published by
Pisces Publications for The Royal Society for the Protection of Birds
The Lodge, Sandy, Bedfordshire SG19 2DL, England

ISBN: 978 1 874357 47 6

Designed by
NatureBureau, Newbury, UK
Pisces Publications is the imprint of NatureBureau

Printed by
Information Press, Oxford, UK

Note: This book has been supported by the UK Government through the Overseas Territories Environmental Programme, as part of the UK Government's commitment to conservation and the protection of biodiversity in the UK's Overseas Territories. The opinions expressed in this guide do not necessarily reflect the views of the British Indian Ocean Territory Administration or the UK Government.

Contents

Foreword

The UK's Overseas Territories are of immense global importance for biodiversity. Together they host over three hundred threatened species and many sites recognised as global conservation priorities. The British Indian Ocean Territory, both the islands and the territorial waters, is no exception.

The British Indian Ocean Territory with 55 islands spread over 10,000 km^2 support some of the most intact and important tropical reef systems and deep sea environments in the world. This rich and productive marine system supports healthy populations of seabirds and 10 islands of the archipelago are currently recognised as Important Bird Areas, with internationally significant breeding colonies – some of the largest and most diverse in the Indian Ocean.

In recent years the work of a handful of birdwatchers and scientists has advanced the knowledge and understanding of the birds. They have documented the breeding species and migrants that regularly winter on the islands and have recorded an array of vagrants well outside their normal ranges. This book compiles this knowledge, with the aim of informing and inspiring further study and the conservation of the birds and their island environments.

Colin Roberts CVO,
HM Commissioner,
British Indian Ocean Territory

Acknowledgements

Albeit this is a short and uncomplicated bird book, there have been many people involved in its production. For its genesis, I would like to thank the Overseas Territories Environmental Programme of the UK Foreign & Commonwealth Office for the grant that made publication possible and Sarah Sanders of the UK Overseas Territory desk in the RSPB for initially backing the concept and assuming ownership of the responsibility. This task was latterly passed to James Millett who continued the sterling support on behalf of the RSPB.

Several people have been generous enough to contribute, free of charge, photographs that have greatly enhanced the book. For their photographic contributions I would like to sincerely thank Chris Patrick, Janet Prushansky, Ian Lewis, Steve Copsey, Mark Cutts, Andy Williams, Nestor Guzman, Mike Watson (Birdquest), Neil Cheshire, Claire Jones, Martyn Dorey, Zoë Townsley, Roger Dickie, Ted Morris, Jean Evans, Glen Tepke, Nigel Phillips, Richard Jeanne, Derek Wilby, Derek Osborn/RSPB and Amelia Dubec. I would also like to thank Chris Burr for technical assistance with the diagrams and maps.

Fieldwork is always a pleasure. Fieldwork on tropical islands, be it conducting censuses of seabirds or puzzling over the latest vagrant wader, is heightened pleasure. Add to this mixture great company and the key to happiness is turned. I have been most fortunate in having the company of good friends and some excellent birders and photographers whilst working on this book. My sincere thanks go to all of the Royal Navy Birdwatching Society/Army Ornithological Society members who joined me on the three expeditions between 1997 and 2007, particularly Chris Patrick, a man of patience, an experienced birder and skilled photographer who took part in all three. Between 2008 and 2010 whilst stationed on Diego Garcia, I was most fortunate to be joined in the field by Janet Prushansky, a talented wildlife photographer and Commander Christopher Moorey RN, the then British Representative, a diligent and enthusiastic birder. The Captains (Neil Sandes and Paul Cragg) and crew of the BIOT Patrol Vessel, Pacific Marlin, were outstanding in all aspects of the service they provided when visiting the outer islands.

Proof reading is not a pleasure! Several people have taken the time and trouble to read some or all of the draft pages of this work and pass comment. For bearing the brunt of this onerous task I would like to sincerely thank Professor Charles Sheppard, Zoë Townsley and James Millett. An unsung task completed with diligence. I would particularly like to thank Professor Chris Feare for his comments and suggestions, the book is better for them.

Finally I would like to thank my wife Anne for having true courage when faced by adversity and the strength of character to allow me to live and work in the Chagos in order to follow my dreams.

Visiting the British Indian Ocean Territory

The British Indian Ocean Territory (BIOT) is a British Overseas Territory. There is no British diplomatic or consular representation in the Territory which is administered from London. Access to Diego Garcia is only permitted to those with connections to the military facility. You will require a permit in advance if you intend to visit any of the outer islands of the Territory. The BIOT Administration in the Foreign and Commonwealth Office in London is responsible for issuing permits. For further information, please check the travel advice for BIOT on **www.fco.gov.uk** or contact **BIOTAdmin@fco.gov.uk**.

CHAPTER ONE

The British Indian Ocean Territory: introduction

"As we coasted along this island, it seemed very fair and pleasant, exceeding full of fowl and coconut trees; and there came from the land such a pleasant smell as if it came from a garden of flowers." (Sir James Lancaster, c. 1602 – on encountering an Indian Ocean island)

The history of the Chagos Archipelago, now the British Indian Ocean Territory (BIOT), follows an all too familiar tale of once pristine oceanic islands being environmentally ravaged following the settlement of man. The twist in the tale for BIOT, however, is that through a unique set of circumstances (and greater global events permitting) the story could have a happy ending for the areas' environment.

Young in geological terms and lying at the southern end of the Lakshadweep-Maldives-Chagos ridge in the geographical centre of the Indian Ocean, the BIOT atolls are as far away from continental land masses as is possible in this ocean. The total area over which BIOT's reefs and shallow areas extend is c. 60,000km^2, but only a tiny fraction of this appears above the surface of the ocean. Due to its recent formation, remoteness, small size and, possibly, lack of altitude, speciation has not been achieved as it has in other island groups, such as Hawaii or the Seychelles: an island group in the same ocean, approximately the same latitude and similar degree of remoteness. However, despite a lack of endemism, there is now a realisation that BIOT offers a unique asset unlike anything else globally; it is a source of marine and avian species that can repopulate the pauperised ecosystems of the Indian Ocean surrounding it.

BIOT has escaped many of the environmentally catastrophic events that the surrounding continental littoral areas of Africa, Asia and Malaysia have suffered. Industrialisation and infrastructure development

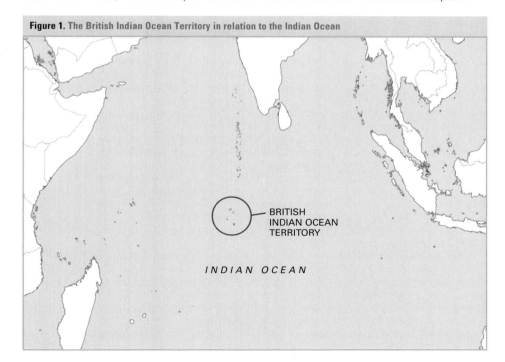

Figure 1. The British Indian Ocean Territory in relation to the Indian Ocean

BRITISH
INDIAN OCEAN
TERRITORY

INDIAN OCEAN

never took place in the days of habitation, and therefore the islands escaped the environmentally damaging effects of mass pollution. The development and degradation caused by over-population was never suffered here. Unlike many of the coastlines and islands of the Indian Ocean, the loss of habitat to tourism did not occur. In comparison to the west, north and eastern shores of the Indian Ocean, BIOT has escaped the major impacts of man's encroachment.

However, after some two hundred years of man's presence, the atolls have nevertheless suffered some deleterious effects. Historically, plantation workers introduced cats, dogs and pigs, and supplemented their diets with seabirds, turtles and other wildlife. The inhabitants would have been at best, partially responsible for the loss of the huge seabird colonies reported on Diego Garcia. It is likely there were also large seabird colonies on the other atoll groups in BIOT but these too have disappeared without trace. Man's lasting legacy to BIOT that still drastically affects the ecology of all of the atolls, is the presence of introduced invasive species, particularly rats, and the severe limitations placed upon biodiversity by the domination of the former coconut crop.

In the two centuries when the atolls were farmed for coconuts, native trees were felled and replaced by a monoculture of coconut palms. Many of the native hardwoods were previously used by breeding seabirds, particularly Red-footed Booby, two species of frigatebird and Lesser Noddy. Replacing these native trees with stands of coconuts deprived at least these species of seabirds of their breeding platforms. These dense, overgrown coconut plantations have caused "coconut chaos": suppressing light underneath their canopy that prevents growth; they eventually kill off most life beneath them. The loss of diversity in trees, plants and shrubs within the coconut chaos would have gone hand-in-hand with the loss of other species, particularly insects dependent on the native plants.

Black Rats were also introduced by man and this had just as great or even greater impact on the delicate atoll ecosystems. Omnivorous and prodigious breeders, they were likely to be a large factor responsible for the loss of huge colonies of the more delicate ground breeding seabirds, such as noddies. Rats on the now uninhabited atolls act as suppressants to bird and vegetation regeneration. Terrestrial nesting seabirds such as Brown Noddy are unlikely to return to the rat-infested atolls and the native hardwood trees struggle to regenerate where they remain, as their seeds are eaten. Rats are indeed recognised as being the major factor in hampering the rejuvenation of the atolls to their "pre-human" natural state. One unsuccessful attempt was made in 2006 to eradicate rats from Eagle Island.

This rather bleak island condition does have one environmental ray of hope shining through: islands within BIOT, with the exception of Diego Garcia, have been uninhabited for over 40 years. The coconut industry declined globally in the 1970s, being replaced by the more commercially viable palm oil grown in enormous quantity in Southeast Asia in particular, and the collapse of the copra industry was a factor in the human populations vacating the northern atolls in the middle of the 20th century. Two plantations, one on Eagle Island and the other in the Egmont Islands were vacated for socio-economic reasons prior to that. In some respects the cessation of maintaining plantations is giving the environment the opportunity to recover to a more natural state but, as noted, this rejuvenation is hindered by rats and is not achievable in dense, former coconut plantations where coconut chaos now reigns.

The rejuvenation process is proving beneficial to more than just the birds. The endangered Hawksbill and Green Turtle now nest undisturbed throughout BIOT where sandy beaches occur. The unusual Coconut Crab, another species of global conservation concern, is present in healthy numbers where illegal poaching by organised groups or visiting yachts has not impacted. Underwater, BIOT is world renowned, having the cleanest sea water recorded in the 21st century, with coral reefs that are used by scientists as control standards against which to measure other reefs of the world.

Some of the islands of BIOT are named after seabirds and this is likely to be indicative of former distribution. However, the lack of historic counts of the avifauna, particularly the globally important seabird colonies, means that only data from the past 30 years can be analysed for population trends. It is known that in the early 1970s there were very few seabirds breeding on mainland Diego Garcia. Subsequent to most of the eastern arm of the island being placed out of bounds, seabirds have returned; by 2005, there were some 3,500 breeding pairs of Red-footed Booby. Similarly, in 1996, there were no Red-footed Booby breeding in the Salomon Islands; by 2010 (re)colonisation had occurred on four of the islands in this group and the breeding numbers appear to be increasing annually. Comparable events can be seen in the Egmont Islands; by 2010,

Figure 2. The terrestrial atolls and major isolated islands of the British Indian Ocean Territory

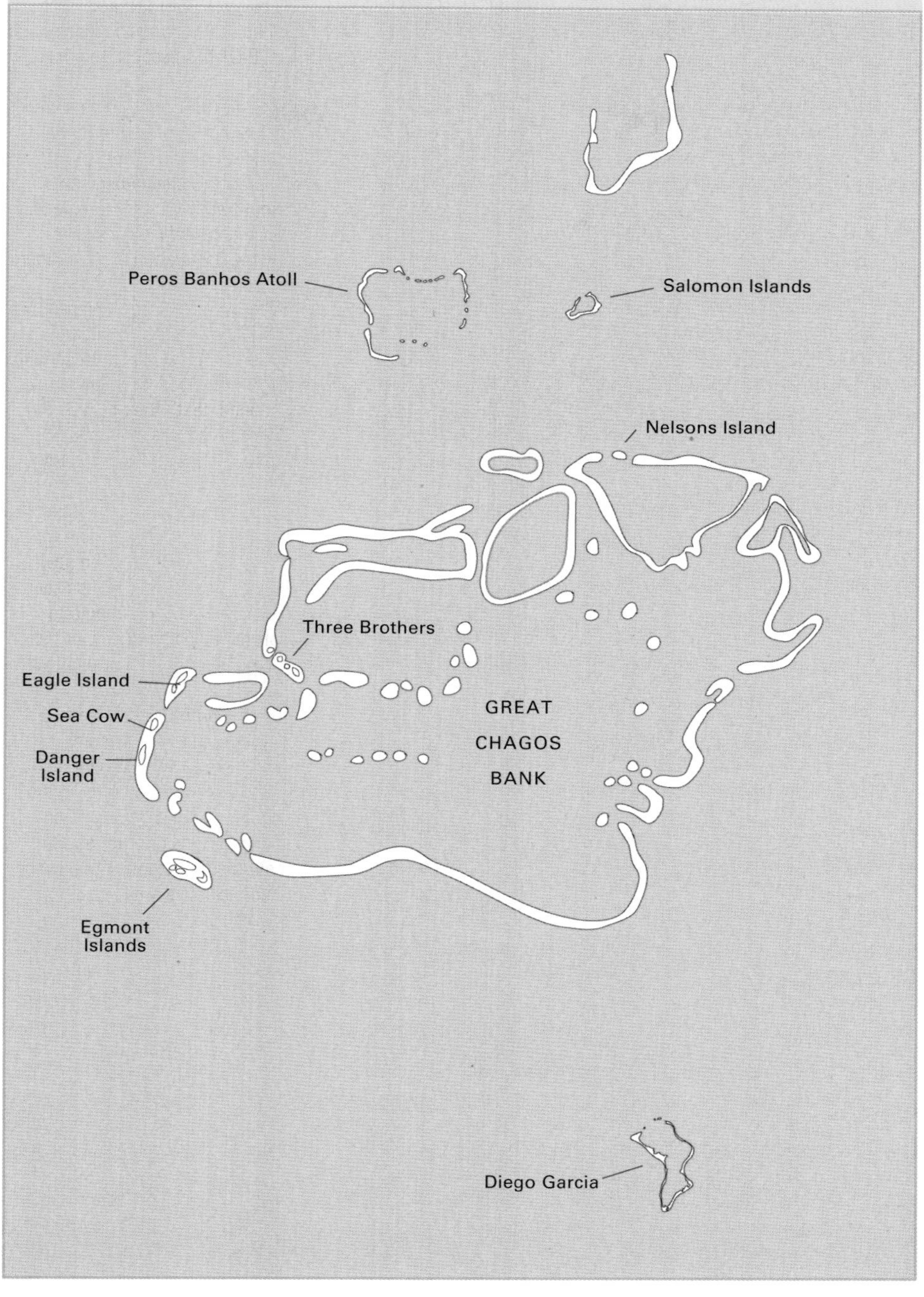

Peros Banhos Atoll

Salomon Islands

Nelsons Island

Three Brothers

Eagle Island

Sea Cow

Danger
Island

GREAT

CHAGOS

BANK

Egmont
Islands

Diego Garcia

rat-infestation notwithstanding, the robust Red-footed Booby has established a small breeding colony on the largest island of Ile Sudest, in the remaining coastal hardwood trees.

Due to the absence of historic data and because of restricted access imposed upon many of the atolls, several ornithological mysteries still remain. These mysteries are crucially important when constructing conservation management plans. An understanding of the internationally important seabird colonies' breeding strategies is imperative to their conservation. For some species, such as Sooty Tern and Brown Noddy, it is not fully understood on which islands they breed. It is known that they breed on certain islands, but whether they breed on the same islands annually or, swap islands on some random rotational basis is not yet known.

Another enigma lies in which months the seabirds breed. Some populations appear to be annual breeders, having a protracted breeding season generally between November and April, as in the case of both shearwaters. Others appear to breed continuously but have spikes in their breeding populations, such as with the boobys. Species such as Brown Noddy breed all year round in low numbers in trees but also nest in their thousands on the ground at, as yet, undetermined periods. Finally, with the Sooty Tern, one of the most prolific breeding birds in BIOT, there is no comprehension of its breeding timings at all. Most likely it breeds on a sub-annual basis as is the case on Ascension, alternating which islands are used as breeding grounds in different years.

Diego Garcia itself is an oddity in BIOT. By far the largest landmass, with an anthropocentrically corrupted ecology, it is home to the majority of introduced species. Since the 1970s it has been considerably developed on its western arm. This development has substantially altered the composition of the flora and fauna of the atoll and is unlikely to be reversed in the foreseeable future. Changes to the landscape have, however, greatly increased the diversity of habitat and have increased the opportunity for bird biodiversity. With the growth of man-made wetlands such as sewage plants, the numbers of birds such as White-winged and White-cheeked Terns, has increased. Other species such as Common Moorhen and White-breasted Waterhen have colonised naturally and have found suitable enough habitat to allow them establish breeding populations.

The presence of a semi-permanent human population on Diego Garcia, some with an interest in birds, has led to a rise in the number of species in BIOT being recorded. A visit by eight ornithologists from the United Kingdom Royal Navy Birdwatching Society in November 2007 produced 15 new species for the Territory. Without doubt, many more northern hemisphere overshooting migrants are destined to be found by a keen-eyed birdwatcher.

Looking longer-term, the total demise of the atolls through global warming and the rise in sea-levels is a distinct possibility, but in the short-term, with conscientious environmental management aimed at restoring the native vegetation on at least some islands, as is being done in Seychelles, the flourishing of the flora and fauna of BIOT, particularly its seabirds, looks promising. With so many of the seabird populations in the Indian Ocean drastically being reduced through anthropomorphic interference, the saving grace for Indian Ocean seabirds could be the atolls of BIOT: a potential reservoir of oceanic species capable of repopulating the surrounding impoverished areas once conservation priorities and policies are set in place.

CHAPTER TWO

Man's impact on the avian populations of the British Indian Ocean Territory

"Islands are typically species poor for their area in comparison to areas of mainland, and this poverty is accentuated by increasing isolation and decreasing island relief and altitude." (Whittaker, 1998).

The biota of true oceanic islands, those located over an oceanic plate that has never been connected to a continental land mass, is influenced by several factors: isolation, area, relief and altitude are important amongst these. Age is also a major factor: the longer an island has been in existence, the greater the opportunity for events to occur that affect speciation.

The 50 or so islands in the five islanded atolls that now form the British Indian Ocean Territory are good examples of true oceanic islands. Situated in the central Indian Ocean, over 2,000 km from Africa, Indonesia and mainland Asia, they are, and have always been, isolated. Diego Garcia, the largest land mass in BIOT and over 10 times the size of any other island, is a mere 2,700 ha. The average maximum height of the atolls of BIOT is just three metres above sea level, though a few locations in Diego Garcia reach about seven metres where sand dunes have consolidated. The islands that form the Chagos Archipelago today are only a few thousand years old which is a miniscule lifespan in evolutionary terms. All these elements combine to give the area a naturally impoverished variety of habitats and hence of avifauna.

The weather systems throughout BIOT are fairly dependable. The area very rarely feels the full force of cyclones, though severe storms do occur that readily fell trees and impact upon shorelines. From October to April winds are normally from the north-west and are light to moderate; for the rest of the year the Southeast trades blow strongly. Rainfall is marked, with most falling between October and April, the northern atolls being wettest with up to 4,000 mm per annum. The daily temperature averages around 27°C.

The waters of the Central Indian Ocean are generally poor in nutrients, though there is some evidence of increased nutrients and productivity around BIOT. This phenomena remains under-researched and in need of investigation. It is known that the waters of BIOT are little affected by anthropogenic contaminants and in comparison to other marine areas are pristine.

Historic impact on avian populations in BIOT

Historically, man's influence on the avian populations of oceanic islands globally, particularly the seabirds, has been catastrophic. The same destructive impact on birds has certainly been felt throughout the Indian Ocean. This destruction in the Indian Ocean has occurred through seabird harvesting; the negative influences of introduced species; the replacement of natural habitat by coconut plantations and the destruction to habitat caused through guano mining. In addition, in many Indian Ocean islands, has been the recent destruction of natural habitat caused by the development of islands for tourism or, in the case of Diego Garcia in BIOT, as in a few other Indian Ocean islands, for military purposes.

BIOT has suffered the same detrimental effects as other Indian Ocean islands in relation to its bird populations. Since the French first colonised the area in the late 1700s, the culling of birds, particularly seabirds, has been employed to supplement diets. Indigenous flora, particularly hardwoods, that are an important nesting platform for Red-footed Booby and Lesser Noddy, have been removed either for export, construction or to make way for coconut plantations. Some invasive animals have been introduced by man, amongst which are rats, feral cats and pigs. All of these have had a vastly detrimental effect on the atoll and island ecosystems, with the terrestrial nesting seabirds suffering the most.

What is immediately evident when approaching any island in BIOT from the sea is whether or not it was ever inhabited. Those islands cleared of native trees and set up as coconut plantations appear dark, lifeless and uniform: Eagle Island is a classic example of these circumstances. On such islands, a walk through the stands of coconuts reveals what appears a sterile and empty habitat, with the only life evident being the ubiquitous rats. The dense, closed coconut canopy does not allow other plants to survive underneath. Native seeds that are trying to sprout in the gloom against all odds are likely to be eaten or destroyed by rats.

The air above such islands is still – broken only by the occasional call of a Brown Noddy, nesting alone high up in the coconut fronds, away from the predatory rats. Common White Tern, which also nests individually, is one of the few beauties of nature to visit these impoverished areas, as they perform their "synchronised" paired courtship display flights above the islands. The only other birds likely to be seen in this habitat are chickens. Some of these birds are survivors from the plantation days, while others may have been introduced by poachers as a future food source. The relict plantations are dark and inhospitable, and contribute very little to the avian biodiversity of an island.

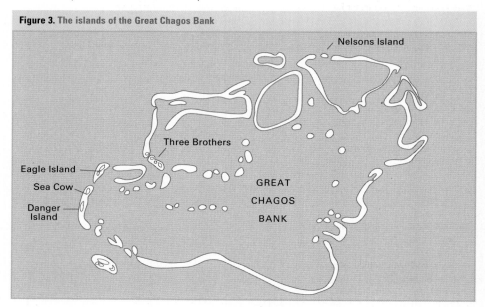

Figure 3. The islands of the Great Chagos Bank

The smaller islands near Eagle Island on the western side of the Great Chagos Bank are a stark contrast. For example Sea Cow, which was never permanently settled and is rat free, is a magnificent, healthy and flourishing island. This is evident in the number of boobies, frigatebirds and noddies and, the near lack of invasive plants that the island supports. The nearby virtually unspoilt and rat free Three Brothers group also provide a marked and poignant contrast between lifeless, "coconut controlled" islands, to teeming, open-canopied, hardwood dominated islands or, in the case of a 'fourth brother, called Resurgent, a colony of Masked Boobies.

The old, native forest on (particularly) North Brother, and the other unspoilt islands on the Great Chagos Bank (Middle and South Brother, Sea Cow, Danger and Nelsons) bustle with life. When approaching these islands, the air is full of birds, circling and calling. On landing on the beaches, the cacophony of calling birds can be deafening in peak breeding season. Male frigatebirds can be seen inflating their crimson gular (throat) pouches and holding their wings out spread, giving their incredible courting "American-Indian war cry" in an attempt to attract a mate to their nest. Mating Red-footed Booby bray like donkeys at each other as they tussle over nest sites and material. Inquisitive juvenile Red-footed Booby swoop down to inspect visitors, often trying to land on their heads or camera tripods.

The original flora of these unspoilt (and the environmentally altered) islands of BIOT is thought to have been composed of about 45 species of higher plant, this figure had increased to over 280 by 1996; mostly through deliberate and accidental introductions. The number of higher plant species on any given island is related to the size of the island and the amount of human disturbance it has received. Diego Garcia being by far the largest island and the heaviest populated has the largest plant list, that has greatly increased through introductions since the building of the military facility in the early 1970s.

Away from Diego Garcia, on islands that were not environmentally altered for coconut production, much of the original flora remains. These undisturbed islands are each unique in their vegetation distribution and plant associations, though there are some general themes. The shoreline is often inhabited by the shrub *Scaveola taccarda*, known as Scavvy, or less often the Beach Heliotrope tree. Interspersed amongst these low-growing pair are often naturally occurring coconuts and Guettarda. On larger islands the shorelines are often lined and overhung by the grand native hardwoods, Cordia, the Fish Poison Tree and Takamaka, that occasionally, particularly on exposed headlands are joined by Pisonia. These shoreline native trees provide roosting and breeding sites for Red-footed Booby and are spectacular to see, smell and hear.

Inland other native trees that can be encountered are the Lantern Tree, often associated with Birds Nest Fern, and, Neisosperma, a favoured breeding platform for Lesser Noddy. Some islands have extensive open areas that are either bare limestone or have a covering of grass, these are the areas where Brown Noddy and Sooty Tern breed in their thousands. On North Brother there are low limestone cliffs full of crevices that Audubon's and Wedge-tailed Shearwaters breed in.

On Diego Garcia, the best documented of all the Chagos atolls, there were huge seabird colonies up until the beginning of the 20th century. This is known through the records of visiting scientists around that time and also through the records of commercial guano exportation companies that, as late as 1957, were operating guano mining from the north-eastern sector of the atoll: the area that is now "downtown" Diego Garcia. It can logically be assumed that prior to man's arrival, all of the atolls of BIOT were teeming with breeding seabirds.

Introduced species of birds are another prominent feature of man's colonisation. Diego Garcia, being the largest and historically most populated atoll, suffers the greatest effects from avian exotic aliens. Birds were introduced as a food source, e.g. Domestic Fowl (chickens) and a guineafowl, (likely Helmeted Guineafowl): the guineafowl now being extinct. Chickens forage far and wide on Diego Garcia and it is likely they suppress regeneration of native plants by their thorough "scratching" technique of feeding. Their suppression of regeneration is of particular concern on the uninhabited northern atolls. How this species arrived on islands that were never permanently settled, such as Danger, Sea Cow, Nelsons and Middle Brother, is something of an enigma. Their impact upon seed growth, although not scientifically proven to be detrimental, is likely to be negative.

Cattle Egret was introduced to Diego Garcia in the 1950s as a natural control measure of insect pest species. They are now controlled themselves because they are a hazard to planes using the airfield. This species no longer breeds on mainland Diego Garcia, probably because their nests were destroyed in an effort to prevent numbers increasing. They now nest on the safe havens of East and West Islands where their populations appear to be increasing annually. Globally successful as a coloniser, Cattle Egret has spread from Diego Garcia and is now often recorded on Nelsons Island and in the Egmont Islands. It is of no surprise that this species, which habitually feeds in open areas, frequents Nelsons Island: an island that was not converted into a coconut plantation and still has open, grassy areas. The affect that these predators have on terrestrial nesting terns is known to be deleterious and if they successfully colonised the northern atolls could severely impact on the breeding Black-naped Terns and the miniscule Roseate Tern population.

Other species such as House Sparrow, Common Myna and Madagascar Red Fody were most likely introduced as pets, or possibly released to become reminders of home or, with Common Mynas, as an agent of anticipated pest control, as described for Cattle Egrets above. The sparrow, which historical records suggest was only ever found on Peros Banhos and the Salomon Islands, appears extinct. It may have been out-competed by the ecologically similar fody or needed man to be present to survive. The myna is now only resident on Diego Garcia: it has been reported as being found, up until the early 20th century, on the then inhabited Egmont Islands too. In all probability, this species is likely to be dependant on man and man-made habitat in BIOT for its long-term survivability. Of all of these introduced birds, the fody has been the most successful and has spread to all of the islands in BIOT which are not completely covered in coconuts.

House Crow is the most recent and unwelcome possible permanent addition to the BIOT avifauna. Almost certainly arriving via a visiting ship, by 2009, two birds were resident on Diego Garcia. All efforts are now being made to eradicate this invasive pest before it can establish a viable population in the Territory. These two birds were found extremely infrequently in 2010 and may have died or departed.

Birds are not the only damaging addition to the introduced species inhabiting BIOT. Along with the historic animal introductions mentioned in the introductory chapter – Cane Toad and an agamid lizard, commonly known as the Bloodsucker, have both appeared on Diego Garcia in the past decade. Neither is welcome. Both of them would have arrived in the cargo of visiting merchant ships; the diet of both species is not known on Diego Garcia and both are likely to impact destructively on the indigenous flora and fauna.

The other major man-made impact on the biodiversity of BIOT has been the creation of a military base on Diego Garcia, with all its associated infrastructure. Much of the north-western area of this island has been developed from a working plantation to something reminiscent of a small United States town. This development has entailed the creation of sewage farms; the digging of drainage ditches; the clearing of coconut groves into open, grassy spaces; and the operating of a rubbish dump. Whilst none of this modernisation can be viewed as aesthetically pleasing, it has established a mosaic of habitats. Birds have been attracted to these new habitats since the military build up began in the early 1970s. New species such as White-breasted Waterhen and Common Moorhen have naturally colonised and established small resident populations. Other new species of regular northern hemisphere winter migrants are also attracted to the artificial wetlands: Common and White-winged Tern are annual visitors to the sewage farms from November through to April. Although not intentional and not in keeping with the natural biodiversity of the area, the development of Diego Garcia has increased the number of bird species to be found there.

The construction and maintaining of a military base on Diego Garcia has brought with it a high proportion of non-indigenous plants and some new insects and a subterranean-inhabiting blind snake. Many of the plants and the insects and, most likely the snake, appeared in the early days of construction and are likely to have been stowaways in aggregates used to build the base. The mistakes of the past have been heeded and there are now strict laws governing the importation of construction materials, as well as robustly enforced laws prohibiting the importing of any flora and fauna.

The military facility on Diego Garcia does bring with it an inherent environmental risk. However, both the terrestrial and marine environment is constantly monitored and policed by both British and US authorities. The lagoon water of Diego Garcia is regularly tested for a variety of potential pollutants and remains extremely clean and has a thriving marine ecosystem. On land, all drinking water comes from aquifers that are usually very close to the surface. Due to the potential of polluting these essential assets and to protect the islands' ecosystems there are very strict laws and codes of practice concerning, for example, the use of pesticides, the management of hazardous material and waste and, spill and pollution prevention. Diego Garcia is a very clean island that in comparison to other similar sized habitations would rank very high for environmental awareness and protection.

Current circumstances in BIOT

As with most other island groups in the Indian Ocean, man's colonisation has altered the ecology of BIOT. Professor Feare in 1984, wrote that the rate of change of habitat by man on most islands in the Indian Ocean has reached a nadir, and, some islands are now being allowed, or even encouraged to revert to their former states. There are a number of important historic factors which give the potential for the avian populations of BIOT today to recover, if greater global environmental events do not impede. The most important of these were the collapse of the copra industry resulting in the depopulation of the northern atolls and also the creation of a military base on Diego Garcia, together with its associated restrictions on visiting the archipelago. A recovery is possible and likely because many of the now uninhabited islands are reverting back to a more natural state and seabirds have the opportunity to colonise them once again – unfettered by man.

The seabirds continue to re-colonise the specific islands that have had access restrictions placed upon them. Of huge conservation interest with regards to the breeding seabirds are the islands that have been placed completely out of bounds to all (with exception of the British military and authorised scientists). For example, on Grand and Petite Coquillage in the Peros Banhos atoll, there have been substantial increases in the numbers of breeding Red-footed Booby and Lesser Noddy over the past two decades, as well as new species colonising, such as Great Frigatebird. In the Salomons, over the same period, Red-footed Booby has started breeding on four islands, with the annual breeding population now over 250 pairs. Comparably, in the Egmont Islands, on the rat-infested Ile Sudest, amongst the few remaining hardwoods that have a tenuous hold on a coastal spot, Red-footed Booby has also established a small breeding population.

Figure 4. Peros Banhos and the Salomon Islands depicting islands where some seabird populations are increasing

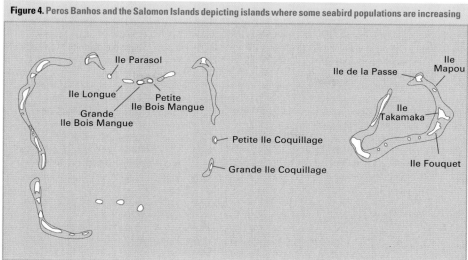

Figure 5. Diego Garcia showing the present breeding colony of Red-footed Booby that stretches from Cust Point ocean-side virtually continuously to Shark's Cove lagoon-side

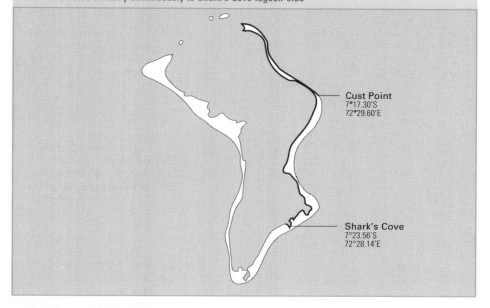

A similar success story has occurred on Diego Garcia. A visionary British Representative in the early 1980s, Commander John Topp RN, placed much of the eastern arm of the island out of bounds to all personnel. At that time, there were very few pairs of Red-footed Booby breeding on mainland Diego Garcia. Nearly 30 years on, there are over 5,000 pairs breeding virtually continuously along the lagoon coast from Shark's Cove up to Barton Point and on to Cust Point ocean-side

The future

If greater global environmental problems do not impede, the continued expansion and increase in the breeding seabirds can be expected. Man has the opportunity to assist with this recovery, if the will and funds can be found. With the declaration of a Marine Protected Area in 2010 and the likely increase in the number of the islands receiving Important Bird Area status as more seabird data becomes available, the will and funds are a strong possibility.

Two major problems will inhibit the seabirds' continued growth in numbers: the rats and the coconuts. If conservation management plans could be agreed and financed (these include long-term strategies of eradicating rats from key islands, together with clearing coconut stands and replacing them with native hardwoods) some of mans' damaging legacy to these unique islands can be reversed, and part of the anthropomorphic harm previously done to the BIOT ecosystems and environment can be repaired. Several successful island restoration projects have been undertaken globally, the methodology employed and benefits to wildlife are well documented; the islands of BIOT display all the necessary hallmarks of islands that deserve top priority in an international arena for investment in restoration.

CHAPTER THREE

Bird conservation in the British Indian Ocean Territory

"Time is not on the side of the Chagos ecosystem."
(Dr Charles Sheppard & Dr Mark Spalding – Chagos Conservation Management Plan, October 2003)

A brief history of conservation and bird recording in BIOT
Conservation of the birds of BIOT has, historically speaking, not been considered important by past governing bodies of the archipelago. Much of the previous wanton destruction of seabird colonies was conducted most likely through ignorance of the consequences, rather than a deliberate attempt at eradication. Whatever the reason, the result has been the same on the birds: their populations dwindled. The same could be said of the hardwood forests that were felled for coconut plantations or the blasting of coral reefs for aggregate for the military installation on Diego Garcia.

There have been some erratic attempts at conservation in the past in BIOT. The control of rats was long employed on the previously inhabited atolls: captured and killed rats being a source of pocket-money for children on Diego Garcia into the 1950s, the children being paid three cents a corpse. Of particular merit are the efforts of the inspired plantation manager James Spurs in the 1870s, who banned his workers from killing seabirds, turtles and coconut crabs until such times as their populations allowed them to be harvested in a sustainable manner. Historic records of enlightened eco-friendly management such as Spurs' are very few and far between.

The richness and global importance of the terrestrial and marine flora and fauna of BIOT started to be discovered in the late 1960s and early 1970s. With the prospect of a military installation being created on Diego Garcia, the late 1960s saw surveys carried out there in several natural history disciplines. In addition to scientists conducting specialist surveys around this period, 1971 saw a seminal publication about the birds of BIOT by Dr Bill Bourne. This work reviewed the scant and scattered literature to that date, tying it together, and remains one of the most important ornithological works on the area.

The outer atolls received their first serious ornithological attention in the early and mid 1970s, when two UK Joint Service expeditions, accompanied by mainly marine scientists, were undertaken. The records of breeding seabirds gathered by the ornithologist Mont Hirons, who served on both expeditions, assisted in selecting which islands became Important Bird Areas (IBAs) over 30 years later.

It was over 20 years after Mont Hirons' pioneering work in the outer atolls before any further significant bird research was undertaken. In 1996 and 2006, scientific expeditions were granted access to BIOT and bird surveys were undertaken on nearly all of the islands in the archipelago. The results from the 1996 survey also influenced the selection of IBAs, and the 2006 data consolidated and expanded our understanding of the global significance of the breeding seabirds and rightly proposed two additional IBAs.

Whilst the outer atolls were receiving attention from visiting scientific expeditions (with additional seabird records coming from passing mariners), birds on Diego Garcia were being more thoroughly recorded by US military contracted scientists and also by service personnel stationed on or visiting the island. The results of these records have been a fairly comprehensive understanding of what species are present on Diego Garcia and at what time of year; the work recorded an increase from 50 recorded species in BIOT in 1975 when Hirons completed his surveys, to over 100 in 2009 (see Chapter Six).

Current bird conservation measures in BIOT
By 2010, there were various categories of protected areas in BIOT. At the time of writing (2010), the full implications of the creation of a Marine Protected Area (MPA) are to be finalised but; this should bring greater protection to terrestrial environments as well the marine. In international standards, the highest recognised protected area is the Ramsar site based on eastern Diego Garcia (Figure 6). "The Ramsar Convention (The Convention on Wetlands of International Importance, especially as Waterfowl Habitat) is an international treaty for the conservation and sustainable utilisation of wetlands, i.e., to stem the progressive encroachment on and loss of wetlands now and in the future..."

Figure 6. Diego Garcia Ramsar Site

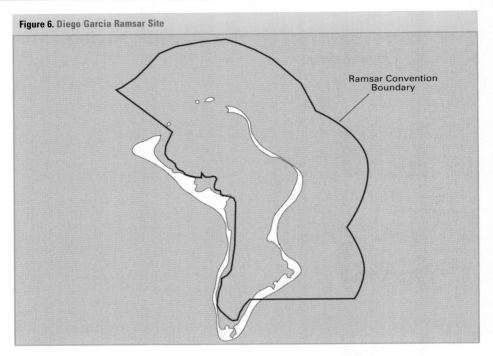

Ramsar Convention
Boundary

Ramsar status equates to the global nature reserve standard of the International Union for the Conservation of Nature (IUCN) category Ia – Strict Nature Reserve: "An area of land and/or sea possessing some outstanding or representative ecosystems, geological or physiological features and/or species, available primarily for scientific research and/or environmental monitoring". Specifically on Diego Garcia, the Ramsar designation was awarded not just because of the outstanding marine life but also because of the number of Red-footed Booby breeding on the eastern arm of the horse-shoe shaped atoll and the three islets in the entrance to the lagoon.

For comparison, sites in the United Kingdom that have Ramsar status are Loch Lomond, the North Norfolk Coast and the Wash and, in the USA, the Okefenokee, the Everglades National Park and Chesapeake Bay – all areas that are recognised for their outstanding beauty and are hugely significant in their contribution to the biodiversity of the region.

Away from Diego Garcia, in the northern atolls are a series of Strict Nature Reserves (Figure 8), decreed by the United Kingdom and with BIOT Laws to enforce any infringement upon them. Landing on any of the Strict Nature Reserves (SNR's) without UK FCO authorisation is a punishable offence under BIOT law, as is sailing within three nautical miles of any of these islands. These reserves are regularly patrolled by British Forces aboard the BIOT Patrol Vessel (BPV), working out of Diego Garcia. These patrols are intended as a deterrent to potential land-based poachers, who harvest from islands the endangered Hawksbill and Green Turtles, Coconut Crabs and birds.

Andy Williams

**The British Indian Ocean Patrol Vessel,
PACIFIC MARLIN**

Figure 7. Strict Nature Reserves in the British Indian Ocean Territory

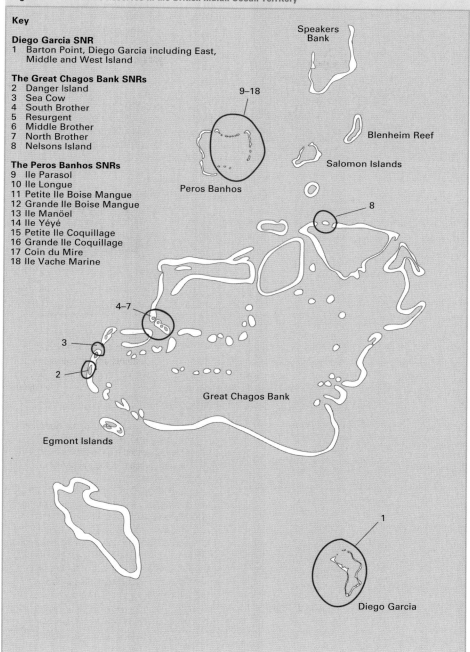

Key

Diego Garcia SNR
1 Barton Point, Diego Garcia including East, Middle and West Island

The Great Chagos Bank SNRs
2 Danger Island
3 Sea Cow
4 South Brother
5 Resurgent
6 Middle Brother
7 North Brother
8 Nelsons Island

The Peros Banhos SNRs
9 Ile Parasol
10 Ile Longue
11 Petite Ile Boise Mangue
12 Grande Ile Boise Mangue
13 Ile Manöel
14 Ile Yéyé
15 Petite Ile Coquillage
16 Grande Ile Coquillage
17 Coin du Mire
18 Ile Vache Marine

BF BIOT

Illegally poached sharks

The BIOT Patrol Vessel also conducts maritime patrols that up until the declaration of the Marine Protected Area, monitored licensed fishing vessels, both long-liners and purse-seiners. Post MPA announcement, it acts as a deterrent for illegal fishing boats and undertakes specific UK FCO tasks. Several illegal fishing boats have been arrested by the Patrol Vessel in the past decade and their haul has always contained large numbers of the ecologically important shark family. Invariably, the poachers are detained, fined and have their fishing equipment forfeited and are subsequently deported. The incidence of illegal fishing has not noticeably dropped since the initial declaration of the MPA and time will tell if possible different strategies employed to police the MPA will make a significant difference.

The Great Chagos Bank SNRs (2–8) are all rat free and are havens for breeding seabirds. Most of them were never permanently settled and were not cleared of their native trees to make way for coconut plantations. The SNRs of Peros Banhos (9–18) are mostly a modern day success story. As with the Great Chagos Bank islands, most of the smaller islands were never settled or converted to coconut plantations and of the islands in the SNRs, only Ile Manöel and Yéyé had were extensively cleared for coconut production –

Table 1. Confirmed and proposed Important Bird Areas in the British Indian Ocean Territory and their qualifying criteria * Denotes a proposed IBA

Site name	Qualifying criteria
Barton Point, Diego Garcia (including East, Middle & West Island)	Breeding Red-footed Booby (4,061 in 2005)
Danger Island	Breeding Brown Noddy (11,100 in 1996) Breeding Red-footed Booby (3,470 in 1996) Congregation of over 20,000 waterbirds
Sea Cow	Breeding Brown Noddy (11,500 in 1996) Congregation of over 20,000 waterbirds
South Brother	Breeding Lesser Noddy (7,300 in 1996) Breeding Brown Noddy (6,100 in 1996) Breeding Sooty Tern Congregations of over 20,000 waterbirds
Middle Brother	Breeding Sooty Tern (12,500 in 1996) Congregation of over 20,000 waterbirds
North Brother	Breeding Audubon's Shearwater (420 in 1996) Over 10,000 pairs of breeding seabirds
Nelsons Island	Breeding Lesser Noddy (13,700 in 1996) Breeding Brown Noddy (8,300 in 1996) Congregation of over 20,000 waterbirds
Ile Parasol	Breeding Sooty Tern (14,000 in 1996) Congregation of over 20,000 waterbirds
Ile Longue	Breeding Sooty Tern (32,000 in 1996) Congregation of over 20,000 waterbirds
Petite Ile Boise Mangue	Breeding Lesser Noddy (12,000 in 1996) Congregations of over 20,000 waterbirds
Petite Ile Coquillage*	Breeding Sooty Tern (34,669 in 2006) Congregation of over .20,000 waterbirds
Grande Ile Coquillage*	Breeding Sooty Tern (15,429 in 2006) Congregation of over 20,000 waterbirds

this is reflected in the lack of breeding seabirds and rat infestation on these. Visiting yachts have not been allowed to anchor or land on any of these islands for several years. Seabird breeding numbers have subsequently increased in the years since their reserve designation and species such as Great Frigatebird now breed on at least one island, Grande Ile Coquillage. Greater global events allowing, there is no reason why the increase in numbers and species should not continue.

In addition to being allocated Strict Nature Reserve status, several of these reserves have also gained Important Bird Area (IBA) status. IBA recognition is given "only if [an island] meets certain criteria, based on the occurrence of key bird species that are vulnerable to global extinction or whose populations are otherwise irreplaceable. An IBA must be amenable to conservation action and management. The IBA criteria are internationally agreed, standardised, quantitative and scientifically defensible. By definition, an IBA is an internationally agreed priority for conservation action." Table 1 details the IBAs in BIOT and why they qualified.

Conservation and Restricted Areas on Diego Garcia

Diego Garcia, with its military establishment, has a unique set of rules governing its use. As well as Restricted Areas in the lagoon, in which boats are not allowed to enter, on land there are also areas with restricted access in order to promote nature conservation. Virtually the entire eastern arm of this island has restricted access and the northern section from East Point Plantation to Barton Point, including the three islets in the mouth of the lagoon are out of bounds to all, unless express permission is granted by the British Representative. Again, this has resulted in a triumph for the birds: when the eastern arm was first closed off in the early 1980s there were but a handful of breeding Red-footed Booby but by 2011 there were over 5,000 breeding pairs, resulting in the creation of the Barton Point Important Bird Area.

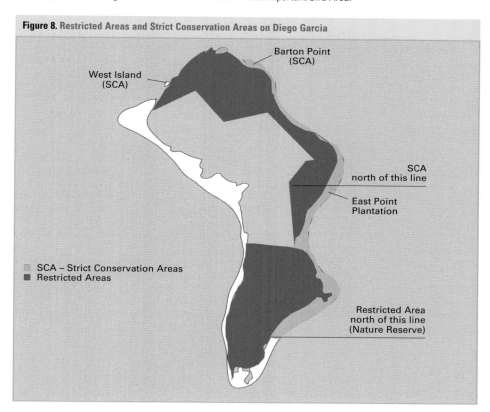

Figure 8. Restricted Areas and Strict Conservation Areas on Diego Garcia

West Island (SCA)

Barton Point (SCA)

SCA north of this line

East Point Plantation

SCA – Strict Conservation Areas
Restricted Areas

Restricted Area north of this line (Nature Reserve)

Future conservation requirements in BIOT

The marine life of BIOT is exceptional. The reefs are considered some of the best in the world and are considered by scientists as the example of what a pristine, undisturbed, unpolluted marine ecosystem should look like. In this respect, the archipelago contains about half of the 'Least Threatened' reefs of the entire Indian Ocean. The marine life of BIOT is also considered globally important as a replenishing resource for impoverished, over-fished and poorly managed marine ecosystems elsewhere in the Indian Ocean.

Whilst the future for avian conservation in BIOT looks promising, with globally important breeding seabird populations apparently thriving, and given the prospect of even greater protection, there are, however, still some important gaps in our knowledge from which conservation management plans can be drawn up.

To successfully conserve birds, a full understanding of their ecological requirements is necessary. This understanding involves more than just the identity and numbers of the birds themselves. Breeding seabirds are dependent, amongst other things, upon food and nesting site availability. The abundance of food, which perhaps varies throughout the year, is likely to dictate breeding times and has a huge effect on fledgling success. Patterns in food availability remain unknown, though because it is known that seasonally changing wind patterns generate different current flows and local upwellings, it is likely that there are also annual variations of marine productivity. Currently, the life cycles of the prey of seabirds in the waters of BIOT and further out in the Indian Ocean is not sufficiently understood. If marine ecosystems are not conserved, the birds will not thrive. Further, if the breeding patterns of the seabirds' themselves are not known or understood, implementing conservation measures to protect them could be misguided or non-beneficial.

Climate change is predicted to bring changes in weather patterns, accompanied by sea level rises. Any significant rise in sea level would have a catastrophic effect on the low lying BIOT atolls and would result in the loss of breeding habitat for the sea birds. More frequent fierce storms may speed up coastal erosion, again causing the loss of breeding habitat and there are indications on some BIOT islands that this is already the case.

There are global events such as climate change looming which will impact upon the pristine waters and protected islands of BIOT. A greater understanding of the potential effects of these global problems is needed in order to establish how they will impact upon the internationally important breeding seabirds of BIOT. If scientific predictions prove true it may be the case, as pointed out in the Chagos Conservation Management Plan; that "time is not on the side of the Chagos ecosystem." This should not preclude the scientific and financial investment required to enhance and preserve this unique resource. Much more scientific research needs to be undertaken in BIOT in order to understand and mitigate the deleterious man-made world-wide problems now affecting this unique area, if the atolls of BIOT are to remain and prosper as seabird havens.

CHAPTER FOUR

Birdwatching in the British Indian Ocean Territory

"The Chagos group occupy a strategic position, not only militarily but ornithologically. They are isolated in the remotest possible position in the tropical Indian Ocean, in a situation lying in the path of both landbird vagrants from three directions, the east, north and west, and seabird migrants from four...." (Dr W.R.P. Bourne, 1971)

Dr Bill Bourne's 1971 quote about the potential capacity for BIOT to pick up vagrant birds from all directions makes the area an exciting spot for bird watching and also a very challenging one. Not knowing whether the unfamiliar wader or tern you have sighted through your telescope has blown in from Africa, Asia, Indonesia or the southern oceans can make identification to species level exacting. Distant views of a hunting falcon, or an accipiter gliding briefly overhead, can be desperately frustrating, as more often than not, the detail acquired in such sightings is not sufficient to make a specific identification. A telephoto lens, an ability to take quality photographs and a good deal of patience has certainly clinched several rarities on Diego Garcia in the past decade.

Vagrants should be expected in BIOT, especially on Diego Garcia (the largest land mass in the Territory), with these birds arriving most frequently in the northern hemisphere autumn. Despite being of little conservation interest, these lost birds do make birdwatching in BIOT very interesting, for example, a pelican and a Greater Flamingo entertained visiting yacht crews in the northern atolls in 2007 and 2009 respectively. Highly migratory, strong fliers are the most likely candidates for vagrancy (though records from the Seychelles indicate poor fliers and non-long distant migrants can also occur) and this leads to the theory that it is only a matter of time before certain families of birds (not yet recorded in BIOT) are sighted: wheatears, pipits and lapwings must be prime candidates on this list.

The number of species recorded in BIOT has risen to over 100 in the 21st century. This figure would certainly increase with more ornithological coverage of the area, particularly among the mosaic of habitats on Diego Garcia. A full list of which species have been recorded in BIOT is available in the next chapter and also on line at [www.worldbirds.org] as well as the Chagos Conservation Trust web-site at [www.chagos-trust.org].

There are restrictions when birdwatching in BIOT, the most obvious being legal access. As highlighted in the previous chapter, only specific islands in certain atolls may be landed upon. Even for those fortunate enough to be working upon Diego Garcia, there are restrictions on access to both the nature reserve and specific areas outside the reserve. The use of cameras and optical equipment anywhere on Diego Garcia is highly inadvisable without first obtaining written permission from the relevant authorities.

The weather is also a constant restriction when birding in BIOT. Daytime temperatures can be extremely hot and dehydration or heat related problems are a real threat. A sun hat, sun block and plenty of drinking water should always be carried when out and about. At the other end of the spectrum, occasional tropical storms do pass through the area and being outside when these occur, especially in the coconut plantations, can be dangerous. Violent squalls are regular at certain times of the year and the amount of precipitation that falls is completely sufficient to waterlog and destroy non-protected photographic or optical equipment.

With these caveats in mind, what follows is a brief description of the birdwatching potential in the various atolls. The final section in this chapter will concentrate on the best birding sites on the vagrant hotspot of Diego Garcia.

The islands of the Great Chagos Bank – Danger, Sea Cow, Eagle, The Three Brothers, Resurgent and Nelsons

With the exception of the rat-infested, coconut plantation-gone-wild, sterile island of Eagle, all of the islands on the outer edge of the Great Chagos Bank are magnificent examples of virtually unspoilt tropical seabird havens. The only glaringly obvious evidence of man on all of the Strict Nature Reserves and Important Bird Areas of the Chagos Bank is the shoreline debris that, even in these remote spots, turns up in vast quantities (literally tonnes).

Access to all of these islands is denied, except to those tasked with checking for poaching and also authorised visiting research scientists. There are no landing facilities on any of the islands and getting ashore invariably entails navigating a very small craft through dangerous channels in the fringing coral reef, followed by an exhilarating swim through strong currents and crashing surf on to, one hopes, a rock free beach. The military parties patrolling the area use life-jackets when swimming ashore to conduct their island inspections. North Brother is notoriously difficult to swim on to, only having two very small sandy spots to beach oneself upon, and the rocky raised limestone reef of Resurgent is only for the powerful swimmer who can boulder-climb – and then only in calm seas.

A typical sight of birds soaring above the Three Brothers, in this case Sooty Terns over Middle Brother in June 2009

On all of the islands of the Great Chagos Bank, Common White Tern, Red-footed Booby, Brown Noddy and Lesser Noddy can be found all year round, the first three breeding in any month, with Brown Noddy doing so individually in trees. There can be thousands of birds present here in the breeding season (dependant upon the species) but, as noted, this does not apply to Eagle Island. Sooty Tern and Brown Noddy breed in open grassy areas and under scavvy in their thousands on most of the islands in most years; the exact breeding season for these two species has still to be ascertained. Visiting these colonies when breeding is in full swing is a sensation to all of the senses, never to be forgotten. Lesser Noddy nest in trees (in species other than coconut which offers very few nesting platforms) and there can be literally hundreds of nests in a single tree. This species is incredibly inquisitive and will drop from its nest and hover in front of you like a huge dragonfly, often only feet away from your face. Where they nest in dense concentrations in interlocking ancient hardwood trees, the scene becomes cathedral like: dark and domed. Only the powerful smell of guano underneath these natural "churches" reminds us that it is used by seabirds and not worshippers.

The barren raised limestone reef called Resurgent

A Lesser Noddy "church"

Occasional pairs of Bridled Tern breed in holes and crevices in raised limestone on most of the Great Chagos Bank islands and Great Crested and Black-naped Terns are regular on all and likely breed sporadically on some stony beaches of the islands. Roseate Tern is very rare in BIOT and breeds in very small numbers, the best sites for these are Resurgent and Coin de Mire. Little Tern can also be found occasionally on these islands in small flocks of less than 20 and, again, breeds in very small numbers.

North Brother, Nelsons and Danger hold small breeding colonies of Brown Booby and up to 600 pairs have been recorded breeding on North Brother but their peak breeding season is still to be ascertained. These magnificent birds peer docilely from their leafy ringed nests on the ground, as a cautious counter treads slowly amongst them. Of the three breeding booby species present in BIOT, Masked Booby is the rarest of this family. Resurgent, an unusual raised reef, holds a modest breeding colony of this ground breeder; the second colony is on the other raised limestone reef of Coin du Mire in Peros Banhos. Both of these islands are virtually vegetation-free and are constantly exposed to all of the elements, seemingly the preferred breeding habitat for this species.

Nelsons also has a well spaced colony of Lesser Frigatebird. To witness the highly vocal and visual courtship display of both Greater and Lesser Frigatebirds, the old Pisonia forest on North Brother is the optimum island. Frigatebirds are klepto-parasites in BIOT of Red-footed Booby and they are found wherever their main hosts are. The number of frigatebirds present is generally dependant upon the number of boobies that are resident on the island.

North and South Brother hold BIOT's largest shearwater colonies, with both Wedge-tailed and Audubon's being present. These pelagic, burrow-breeding species have in places completely honeycombed parts of both islands and walking in such areas is wholly ill-advised for the safety of both birds and walker. Wedge-tailed Shearwater is present in burrows on these islands throughout the year, having a protracted breeding season from November through to May. It was previously thought that this species was only present in BIOT for the breeding season and left the islands as soon as breeding was over: evidence from surveys in 2008 and 2009 indicates otherwise and this species is actually present on the Brothers all year round.

Brown Booby colony on North Brother

Masked Booby breeding on Resurgent, one of two islands in BIOT where this "breeding habitat specific" species nests

Although any island of size in BIOT should expect to see migratory shorebirds, Nelsons Island (which is the most isolated small island in Chagos) is particularly good spot for picking up waders, mainly between November and March. During the northern hemisphere winter, Curlew Sandpiper and Ruddy Turnstone are the most numerous. Most waders return north in April to breed, though Ruddy Turnstone, Whimbrel and Common Greenshank can occasionally be found throughout the northern summer. Nelsons Island is also the only spot away from Diego Garcia where Cattle Egret is regularly viewed. It is presumed that these birds are individuals displaced from the introduced stock on Diego Garcia, as opposed to genuine exploratory vagrants.

Striated Heron has colonised every good-sized island in BIOT and, along with the introduced Madagascar Red Fody, should be expected on all islands on the Great Chagos Bank. The only other species likely to be seen on these islands are chickens. As discussed before, the origin of these birds is debateable but there are small populations on Danger, Sea Cow, Eagle, South and Middle Brother and Nelsons Island.

A wrecked fishing vessel on Nelsons Island

The sandbar that is likely to join Ile Carre Pate to Ile Lubine and then join all of the six Egmont Islands in to one. Between the two sandbars is a stranded ship's boiler

Removing shoreline debris

Pete Carr

Martyn Dorey

The Egmont Islands

The Six Islands as they were once known and thus depicted on historic charts should now be known as the Two Islands. The sand bar between Ile Carre Pate and Ile Lubine, the two remaining land masses, continues to extend towards each other. At its present rate, within 20 years or so the atoll could be called Egmont Island, having by then completely joined up in to one island.

As a result of the old coconut plantations on these islands, which were closed down sometime around 1935, on land this entire atoll has been ecologically devastated by man. Rats are at such a high density that they have become, presumably through necessity, both bold and diurnal, and they are evident everywhere. Coconut trees have been planted densely all over the islands as part of the previous plantation regime and kilometres of these virtually lifeless tracts add nothing to the value of the islands, to man or bird. For reasons unknown, the lagoon facing shoreline of the Ile Lubine group appears to collect shoreline debris at a prolific rate and, as a final anthropomorphic cherry on the atoll's cake, a huge ship's boiler has washed ashore between the two island groups and is very slowly rusting away where the sand bars will eventually meet. This rotting metal hulk is an unsightly reminder that even though man has departed these shores, he still has the capacity to spoil the area.

Hope does glimmer though, even in such spoilt areas. There are a few remaining native trees on the north-western shoreline of both Ile Carre Pate and Ile Tattamucca that were not cut down to make way for the coconut harvest. On these few remaining vestiges of what at one point used to cover the entire islands, Red-footed Booby, the avifaunal ecological indicator of BIOT, has returned to breed. Following the boobies are the frigatebirds. On these two very small coastal strips, nature demonstrates that when given time and left undisturbed, it can heal from the affects of man's environmental mismanagement.

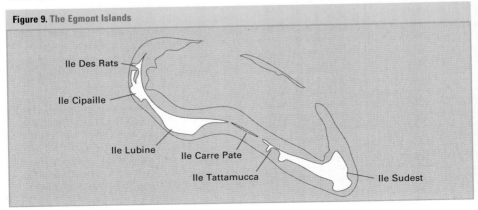

Figure 9. The Egmont Islands

Ile Des Rats

Ile Cipaille

Ile Lubine

Ile Carre Pate

Ile Tattamucca

Ile Sudest

The sandbar that stretches between, but that does not quite join the two island groups, supports breeding Great Crested Tern. These terns nest at no defined period and are always sited well away from the main island. This species appears robust enough to nest on rat-infested islands. In 2009, there were 10–15 pairs breeding in January and again in July. At the end of the sandbars is one of the largest tern roosts in BIOT and any one of the regularly recorded species, including Black-naped, Roseate, Little and Arctic Tern, is likely to be found.

These islands received ornithological attention from a Joint Services expedition that ran from late 1972 through to April 1973. As a result, there are a series of bird records from the atoll unlike anywhere else in BIOT, with the exception of Diego Garcia. Still to date, the only records of Dunlin, Northern Pintail and Little Swift in BIOT are from this atoll. Common Myna was present on this atoll if historical records are correct, though is not present today. The only resident passerine nowadays is the ubiquitous introduced Madagascar Red Fody, and the only other resident non-seabird species on this atoll is the natural colonist, Striated Heron, and introduced chickens.

The coastal strip of Ile Carre Pate, Egmont Islands where Red-footed Booby has returned to breed

Breeding Great Crested Tern in the Egmont Islands

Peros Banhos

Peros Banhos is, ecologically speaking, an atoll of two halves. Including the sandbar island marked as Ile Saint Brandon, which is still very much in the embryonic stage of formation, there are 30 islands in the Peros Banhos atoll. The raised reef of Coin du Mire in southern Peros Banhos is geologically and ecologically different from all other islands in BIOT, except Resurgent. With regards to permitted access onto the different islands, Peros Banhos is divided by a line drawn from the eastern end of Moresby Island in the north through to the eastern tip of Ile Fouquet in the south. All islands east of this line are Strict Nature Reserves and landing on them is prohibited. The islands to the west can be landed upon, though when the wind is blowing from the south-east, such landings from within the lagoon can be hazardous.

Ornithologically, the 19 islands west of the boundary are barren. All of the larger islands this side of the boundary were given over to coconut plantations and all are rat infested. As mentioned in a previous chapter, the only bird of interest that was likely to be seen in this area was the introduced House Sparrow, though even this species (that was apparently never introduced to Diego Garcia) is now extinct.

By contrast, six of the islands in the eastern half have flourishing breeding seabird populations and, as a result, three islands are already Important Bird Areas and two further are proposed (see previous chapter). It is possible that the sixth, Grande Ile Bois Mangue, with further monitoring may also reach the criteria for IBA status. Iles Manöel and Yéyé in the east were environmentally destroyed by rats and hardwood clearance for coconuts during the plantation era and the small island of Ile Vache Marine is rat infested and therefore barren of birds.

The presence or absence of rats in the eastern islands is an interesting question and one that requires answering. A survey in 1996 claimed that every island in Peros Banhos, with the exception of the rock, Coin du Mire, held rats. Extensive trapping and searching for rats in this atoll during 2008 and 2009 suggests that rats are no longer present on Iles Parasol, Longue, Petite and Grande Bois Mangue and Petite and Grande Coquillage. The presence of huge numbers of terrestrial breeding terns and noddies on these islands may be further evidence to substantiate this claim. Four hypotheses have been proposed about the fate of the rats,

Figure 10. Peros Banhos atoll showing the Strict Nature Reserve boundary and the yacht anchorages

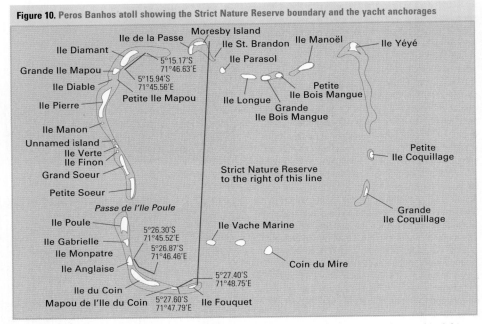

Moresby Island
Ile de la Passe
Ile Diamant
Ile St. Brandon   Ile Manoël   Ile Yéyé
Grande Ile Mapou
5°15.17'S
71°46.63'E   Ile Parasol
Ile Diable
5°15.94'S
71°45.56'E
Petite Ile Mapou   Petite
Ile Longue   Ile Bois Mangue
Ile Pierre
Grande
Ile Bois Mangue
Ile Manon
Unnamed island
Ile Verte   Petite
Ile Finon   Ile Coquillage
Grand Soeur   Strict Nature Reserve
Petite Soeur   to the right of this line
Passe de l'Ile Poule   Grande
Ile Poule   Ile Coquillage
5°26.30'S
71°45.52'E   Ile Vache Marine
Ile Gabrielle
5°26.87'S
Ile Monpatre   71°46.46'E
Ile Anglaise   Coin du Mire
5°27.40'S
71°48.75'E
Ile du Coin
Mapou de l'Ile du Coin   5°27.60'S   Ile Fouquet
71°47.79'E

the first being the original data were not accurate; the second that some virus or disease has rendered these populations extinct or, more likely perhaps, that the populations on these islands were so small that inbreeding over many years has led to their extinction. The fourth hypothesis is that the surveys in 2008 and 2009 simply failed to locate rats that were still present.

The designation of the Strict Nature Reserves in Peros Banhos and the resulting cessation of landings by visiting yachts appears to have vastly benefited the birds. Two surveys of these islands 10 years apart (1996 and 2006) revealed that there has been an increase in breeding numbers of seabirds on these islands. Some species that bred in extremely small numbers, as recorded in 1996, appear to be lost as breeding species to Peros Banhos in the 2006 data. This may be due to the lack of synchronisation of the breeding periods of the species involved between the surveys and also the challenges of recording breeding seabirds rather than due to a local extinction, but overall there have been some major ornithological gains. In 2006, Lesser Frigatebird was found breeding for the first time, and further surveys during 2008 and 2009 showed that Greater Frigatebird has started nesting on Ile Grande Coquillage. As these species are at the top of the food-chain in BIOT and therefore are good ecological indicators, it is presumed that their colonisation demonstrates the healthy condition of these islands.

Sooty Tern, the most numerous of the seabirds in BIOT, nests in its thousands on Iles Parasol, Longue and Petite and Grande Coquillage. The breeding strategy of this species in BIOT is not yet understood, though it is known that not all of the above islands are bred on every year and, the months for breeding do vary between years. These colonies, which are an extraordinary spectacle of nature, undoubtedly once supplied the plantation

Greater Frigatebird and young on Grande Coquillage

workers with a huge dietary supplement in the form of eggs. Nowadays, left undisturbed, they have the opportunity to return to their former numbers, which were reported (at least on Diego Garcia) to be over 100,000 birds at the turn of the 20th century. To ascertain if the numbers are increasing, accurate determination of the breeding regime and monitoring of the colonies is required.

Lesser Noddy breeds in small numbers on most of the eastern islands. In particular, it constructs its delicate arboreal nests in their thousands on Petite and Grande Iles Bois Mangue and Grande Coquillage. Petite Ile Bois Mangue is the premier nesting site for this species in Peros Banhos and probably in the whole of BIOT. The nesting conditions on this island are likely to be a reflection of how this species may have once nested on all islands prior to mans' clearance of the giant hardwoods for coconut plantations. On Petite Ile Bois Mangue there are three "glades" of enormous Pisonia trees in which the birds breed at varying times, each glade holding 5–10 trees; up to 15,000 Lesser Noddy breed in less than 30 trees. These enormous, twisted, ancient trees have intertwined around each other and have formed dark cavernous halls. The pungent smell of guano, the cacophony and the bold inquisitiveness of the birds, make these halls another wonder of nature in BIOT.

Wedge-tailed and Audubon's Shearwater were both claimed to be breeding in small numbers in Peros Banhos in 1996, the former on rat-infested Yéyé. Although neither species was found breeding in 1996, Audubon's Shearwater was found breeding in small numbers on Ile Petite Coquillage in 2009 and Wedge-tailed Shearwater was still breeding on Coin de Mire in tiny numbers in 2010. White-tailed Tropicbird is an incredibly difficult species to prove to be breeding: it probably still nests in the atoll in very small numbers although this can not be said conclusively. It was said to be breeding in 1996 but was not found again in 2006.

As with all of the atolls in BIOT, the greatest ornithological success lies with the booby family. The ground nesting Brown Booby retains a very small breeding population amongst the 100 or so pairs of Masked Booby on Coin du Mire. However, it is Red-footed Booby that has increased in numbers and is colonising undisturbed islands. This species now breeds in varying numbers on all of the eastern islands except the tiny rat-infested Ile Vache Marine and volcanic rock of Coin du Mire. Red-foots are unlikely ever to breed on the latter due to lack of suitable habitat.

All of the islands of any size in Peros Banhos support Madagascar Red Fody and Striated Heron. In January 2009, an Indian Pond-heron had taken up residence in the old plantation area on Ile du Coin: this bird is likely to have arrived as part of the same influx that saw this species first appear on Diego Garcia and the Salomon Islands. As well as the birds, Ile du Coin still has at least one donkey inhabiting it too. Amazingly, the specimen most often seen in 2009 is a sleek jet-black specimen, and is very territorial: it will challenge intruders on the island by coming right out onto the beach, face those alighting from a craft, paw at the ground and bray wildly – quite an imposing sight!

The Salomon Islands

As with the Egmont Islands, the Salomons lost their ornithological importance during the plantation era. The four largest islands of Iles Boddam, Anglaise, Takamaka and Fouquet are all barren, rat-infested former coconut plantations. The latter two are showing some signs of ornithological hope in that Red-footed Booby have started to roost in small numbers in the few remaining coastal hardwoods on Fouquet, and there were also over 250 breeding pairs on Takamaka in 2006. This number of birds breeding on an island regularly visited by yacht crews is extremely heartening, both in the robustness of the birds to disturbance and the apparent sensitivity of the mariners landing.

In 2009, Takamaka hosted a colony of just under 50 pairs of breeding Black-naped Tern on its sandbar facing Fouquet. It is possible that other opportunistic breeders such as Great Crested, Roseate and Little Tern nest on other sandbars of the atoll on an occasional basis.

The "Royal Chagos Yacht Club"

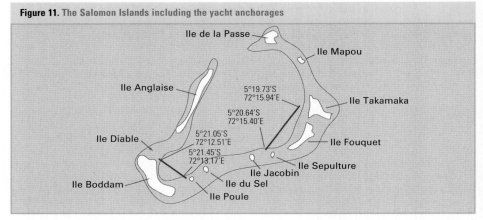

Figure 11. The Salomon Islands including the yacht anchorages

The two other islands of any size, Iles Mapou and Passe, are also showing signs of rejuvenation. Along with the tiny breeding populations of arboreal Brown Noddy and Common White Tern, the past two decades have seen both islands colonised by Red-footed Booby: the Mapou population rising to over 40 pairs by 2009. Mapou also has a small colony of 50 pairs of Lesser Noddy. This island is of additional interest as it hosts a species of gecko, the exact species and its origins being unknown.

Ile Boddam, an island that is regularly landed upon by yacht crews, hosts the "Royal Chagossian Yacht Club". This is a former plantation building, adopted by visiting yachts, that now has a makeshift beach volleyball court outside of it. The plantation buildings on Boddam, although fast decaying, are the best examples left in BIOT (outside of Diego Garcia) of the plantation era way of life. Due to its former headquarters status in the plantation days on Salomon, Ile Boddam is a sterile island with very little to offer a visiting ornithologist, though in 2009, an Indian Pond-heron had taken residence and normally was found hunting in the graveyard.

Along with the few pairs of Common White Tern and Brown Noddy that are present on all islands, Madagascar Red Fody and Striated Heron are also present on the larger islands.

Diego Garcia

Diego Garcia, whose main island contains over half the total Chagos land mass, and being 10 times larger than any other land mass in BIOT, has a mosaic of habitats that includes the only readily accessible and reliable freshwater in the central Indian Ocean. This is the atoll where most species of migrant/vagrant birds will be recorded. Migration plays a significant part in how many birds and what species are present. During the austral winter, Diego Garcia is windy and relatively dry and holds few birds except the resident seabirds, the introduced exotics and the occasional non-breeding wader such as Greater Sand Plover or Pacific Golden Plover As the northern hemisphere autumn migration gets underway, the island becomes populated by regular migrants and over shooting vagrants, mainly from southern Asia. This migratory influx applies to dragonflies as well as birds. By late November, the island is generally laden with ephemeral wetlands, and birds, particularly waders, are much more in evidence.

Throughout October and November, regular migrants such as Ruddy Turnstone, Curlew Sandpiper, Whimbrel, Common Greenshank and Common and Wood Sandpiper start to increase in numbers: the first three reaching numbers in their hundreds. Less numerous but annual waders such as Lesser Sand Plover and Terek Sandpiper put in appearances, normally in the southern barachois. Rarities in BIOT, such as aerobatic Oriental Pratincoles, put in tantalisingly brief appearances too. This species usually remains in BIOT until March, and where these birds disappear to for great tracts of time during their stay is unknown, as sightings of this graceful bird are few. Occasional small flocks of Amur Falcon appear in November and December. These vagrants will have been blown off course from their normal migration route from Southeast Asia to the Madagascar area. Amur Falcon usually only stay on Diego Garcia for a few days: they feed on the ample supply of the dragonfly, normally Globe Skimmer (that seemingly coincides with their arrival), before resuming their journey to East Africa.

Diego Garcia, as Dr Bill Bourne's initial quote suggests, is a mecca for overshooting migrants, particularly from Southeast Asia. There are numerous records of birds that have been recorded to date only once or a very few times. These records cover the entire range of bird families and include oddities such as the Greater Flamingo, photographed and reported from the Salomon Islands by a visiting yacht, through to "expected" overshooting vagrants like Gull-billed Tern and Rosy Starling.

Figure 12. Birdwatching sites on Diego Garcia

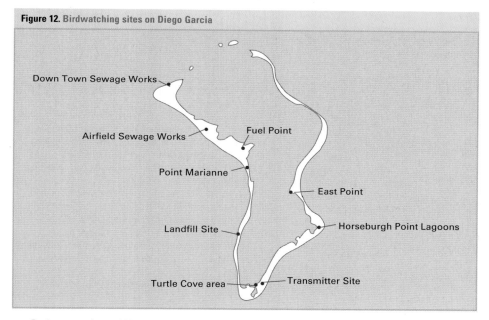

For larger numbers of birds, the southern barachois are always worth checking. This is especially true as the tide advances, reducing the area waders can feed on. Concentrated flocks of feeding waders are worth checking for the oddity amongst them. After rains, when temporary ponds are present, the Landfill Site is excellent for waterbirds: the replanted landfill grasslands at the northern end of this spot are a favoured roosting area for egrets and waders.

The three sewage farms are also havens for birds. At high tide the grassy walkways between the settling ponds act as roosting areas. The edges of the sewage ponds themselves support vast amounts of invertebrates and these in turn attract feeding shorebirds. Particularly common to these spots are Curlew Sandpipers, though all of the ponds have hosted the very rare Little Stint and even the extremely rare Barn Swallow. The Downtown sewage works is the most reliable site for White-winged Tern and this is the only spot where White-cheeked Tern have been recorded. The sewage works nearest the airfield is a regular haunt for wintering Garganey, and was the most reliable site to find the solitary Glossy Ibis that has resided on Diego Garcia for over a decade.

On the airfield side of the vehicular petroleum refuelling site is the premier birding spot on Diego Garcia. This tidal area has a saline reed-bed and tracts of exposed mudflats when the tide is low. Several extreme rarities have been found here including Grey Heron, Great Egret, Little Egret and Grey-tailed Tattler. It is difficult to access and has limited viewing spots, but the effort and muddy feet are generally well rewarded.

It is worth mentioning that during autumn migration, any wet spot or grassy area is worth checking. It is also worth looking up and checking the sky now and again. In November 2007, three species of swift were found in 10 days by a group of visiting UK ornithologists, all found by diligent observers checking the skies.

As a final note on birdwatching on Diego Garcia, little sea-watching from land has been carried out and, if more were undertaken, patterns of seabird movement about the area might become clearer. Limited experience suggests a strong on shore wind moves passing birds closer to Diego Garcia and therefore makes identification easier. On Diego Garcia three sea watch points have been used: both Simpson Point and South Point are extremely productive when winds are blowing on shore; however, Eclipse Point has its true movement of seabirds masked by the constant stream of Red-footed Boobies transiting to and from Barton Point and the three associated islets. Sea-watching from Diego Garcia has produced species seldom recorded in the BIOT, such as Flesh-footed Shearwater and Wilson's Storm-petrel. Cetaceans are often recorded: Spinner Dolphin is regular both lagoon and ocean-side, with the latter also producing occasional sightings of, as yet, unidentified whales.

The following is intended to give more specific guidance on the most productive birdwatching sites on Diego Garcia.

The derelict pier at East Point, which is a regular tern resting site

Site One: East Point
(7°21.138′S, 72°27.905′E WGS84)
East Point is the site of the old plantation headquarters and once the hub of life on the atoll. It is a site of great interest as it still holds much of the former plantation infrastructure and has notice boards depicting what each building's function was. The plantation church has been restored and occasional services are still held there. The carcass of a beached sea-plane, a Catalina, from World War II is also readily accessible. The derelict pier at East Point is a regular tern roost. Roseate Tern and Arctic Tern can be viewed at close quarters here. General access to this area is only allowed on Sundays at a cost of $2, when a bus service is also available. On any other day, written permission from the British Representative is required, as is a vehicle to get there and back.

Site Two: Horsburgh Point Barachois
(7°23.242′S, 72°28.880′E WGS84)
This is the most challenging area on the atoll to survey and requires determination and a good level of fitness. Similar to East Point, as part of the Restricted Area given over to nature, access is only granted to the road to Horsburgh Point on Sundays. Even on open days written permission from the British Representative is required to leave the track and trek through secondary jungle to the lagoons. The entry point to the lagoons is where the road towards East Point is closest to the Horsburgh Point lagoons. A struggle through dense scavvy and relict coconut stands, brings you to the lagoon shore. It is then a matter of walking through soft mud, climbing over raised rock formations and wading through the lagoon itself to survey the area. This is probably the best area on the entire atoll for waders and often holds species not recorded elsewhere, e.g. Common Redshank and Marsh Sandpiper and in 2005, Spotted Redshank. Telescopes are essential for viewing distant birds and water, sun hats and sun block are advisable.

Site Three: The Transmitter Site
(7°25.855′S, 72°26.510′E WGS84)
The "Aerial Farm" is an area of donkey grazed low herbage that contains freshwater pools after rain. Access to the site is open all year, though there are very clear signs warning personnel not to walk among the transmitters because of the potential radiation hazard. The best place to park is alongside the road where the bulk of the transmitters are sited. This is traditionally the optimal site on Diego Garcia for Pacific Golden Plover and is also where two Amur Falcons were recorded in 2002. Telescopes are essential for viewing distant birds. This site can be surveyed from the road without the need for walking.

Site Four: The Southern Barachois
(Barachois Sylvaine covering Turtle Cove)

This barren and unearthly area is both starkly beautiful and very rich in biodiversity. It encompasses all of the barachois at the southern end of Diego Garcia. It is a complex area that is difficult to enter except at Turtle Cove. Access to Turtle Cove is open at all times and two viewing platforms have been erected for visitors to spot turtles, sharks, rays and shoals of fish moving in and out of the barachois. There are notice boards at Turtle Cove informing visitors of the BIOT laws regarding environmental protection in this open area. All other parts of the southern barachois require written permission from the British

Transmitter Site
Turtle Cove
The Southern Barachois and the Transmitter Site

Representative. Movement around anywhere except Turtle Cove is challenging and surveys are best achieved by kayak at high tide. This is a rewarding area holding good numbers of feeding and roosting waders and terns: it is the site where Gull-billed Tern was recorded in 2005.

Site Five: The Landfill Site
(7°21.250′S, 72°25.914′E WGS84)

The Landfill Site, whilst not the most aesthetically pleasing spot in BIOT, is one of the prime birding (and dragonfly) sites and certainly one of the easiest for recording birds. After heavy rains there are a series of pools that attract good numbers of waders and egrets. Birds can be viewed at a relatively close range and only a short distance need be walked. Both the north and south side of the Public Works building should be scanned: the northern grasslands being a favoured roosting area. This site has produced many BIOT rarities such as Common Ringed Plover and Pectoral Sandpiper and it is the most reliable site on the island to see the recently colonised Indian Pond-heron. A word of caution: this is an active waste disposal area and has all of the associated hazards any such site would hold. Permission must be acquired from the relevant authorities on Diego Garcia prior to access.

Part of the Landfill site, an active waste management area that attracts large numbers of waders and egrets

Site Six: Point Marianne and associated Wetlands
(7°19.400′S, 72°25.665′E WGS84)

At the southern end of the runway is an area of natural wetland that is excellent for freshwater-loving species such as Garganey and Wood Sandpiper. In particular, there is a small pond on the lagoon side of the road that is not only a bird magnet during wet periods, it is also probably the best Odonata (dragonfly) site on the atoll. Lesser Green Emperor and Picturewing, both recent additions to Diego Garcia's dragonfly list, are regular here in the austral summer. The lagoon shore at Point Marianne is worth

The Point Marianne wetlands area

Mark Cutts

The reed bed by the vehicle refuelling site, possibly the premier birding site on Diego Garcia for waders and heron species

scanning as it can hold the largest tern roost on the entire atoll. The old Point Marianne plantation is now overgrown, though the buildings housing the leper colony are still in evidence. Just off the main road, the Point Marianne cemetery is kept in pristine condition and is the site of Remembrance Day parades held by British Forces stationed on the island.

Site Seven: Fuel Point Reed Bed (7°18.199´S, 72°24.200´E WGS84)

This site is reached by walking south down the outside of the fence of the vehicular Fuel Point. It is difficult to access and there are few natural viewpoints and much dead ground. Invariably, to get to a good spot to observe the birds, wet and very muddy feet should be expected. However, it is

worth the effort as this is the premier site on the island for herons, the rarer egrets and rare waders. This site turned up BIOT's first Black-crowned Night-heron and also Common Moorhen, now a natural colonist, in 2007. The habitat is brackish water containing some exposed mud, a tidal channel and a dead "reed-bed" of some description. Telescopes are essential to observe distant birds.

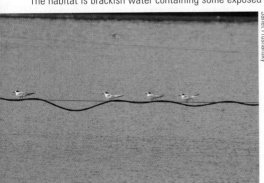

Janet Prushansky

The Airfield Water Treatment Works with terns

Site Eight: The Airfield Water Treatment Works (7°15.237´S, 72°22.159´E WGS84)

This man-made site, containing permanent freshwater, in the austral summer attracts large numbers of easily viewed egrets and waders: it is also one of two favoured sites for White-winged Tern and was the favoured site of the lone Glossy Ibis. No walking is required, telescopes are advisable and permission must be sought and the authorities notified before entering.

Site Nine: The Down Town Sewage Works (7°16.305´S, 72°21.815´E WGS84)

This spot, within walking distance of Downtown, is another man-made site that has permanent freshwater. It is the other favoured locality of White-winged Tern and is the only site where White-cheeked Tern are annual. Other extreme rarities such as Yellow Wagtail, Barn Swallow and Pintail Snipe have been recorded here. The grass walkways are roosting spots and can hold hundreds of birds during the austral summer. The edges of the settling ponds attract feeding waders, Striated Heron and White-breasted Waterhen and flocks of Common Myna also drop in to drink at dusk. Minimum, easy walking is required to cover all of the walkways and telescopes are advisable for distant viewing. Permission must be gained from the United States Navy on Diego Garcia prior to entering the sewage plant compound.

Janet Prushansky

The Down Town Sewage Farm Works with a waders and egrets feeding between the settling ponds

The seas of BIOT

No section on where to watch birds in BIOT would be complete without mentioning the seas of the Territory. The BIOT Economic Exclusion Zone (EEZ) extends approximately from 2°S to 11°S and 68°E to 76°E and these coordinates have been used as the total bird recoding area for BIOT.

Figure 13. The BIOT Economic Exclusion Zone and total recording area for birds

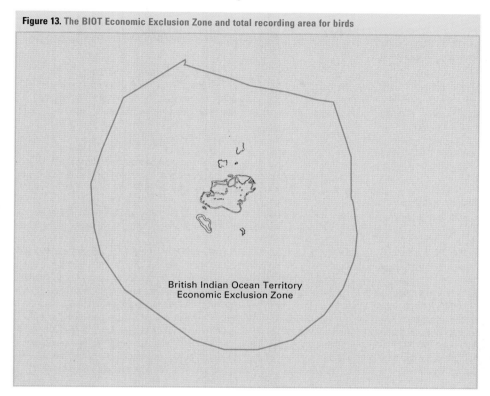

The recording area covers 54,400 km² of ocean and is now the largest Marine Protected Area (MPA) on the planet and is thoroughly under-recorded as to what birds occur. Whilst the seabird species breeding on the 60 km² of land found in the MPA are known and relatively well documented, the seabirds occurring in this mid-Indian Ocean sanctuary are very poorly understood. The limited data to date suggest there is much to be learnt about what species occur, in what months and in what numbers.

The few credible "at sea" records of birds that exist, mainly gleaned from the UK Royal Navy Birdwatching Society (RNBWS) annals, indicate that the mid-Indian Ocean has more seabirds present than is recorded to date, albeit many of these birds may merely be transients. Much more data need to be collected before any meaningful analysis can be conducted and all mariners operating in BIOT waters, be they military, merchant or pleasure seekers, are encouraged to submit there sightings to (at least) www.worldbirds.org.

CHAPTER FIVE

Locating and identifying 50 common birds of the British Indian Ocean Territory

> *"Identifying vagrant species on Diego Garcia has proved very challenging and I am grateful to the manufacturers of digital cameras, big lens's and quality field guides for assistance..."*
> (Pete Carr, 2010)

How to use this section

This chapter gives guidance on the status, favoured locations, expected dates and the identification of 50 species that can be expected to be seen in BIOT. It also contains a brief summary of all birds that have been seen in the Territory.

Species groupings

The avifauna of BIOT naturally divides itself in to three groups: the introduced exotics; the seabirds; and the landbirds, which includes regular migrants, vagrants and natural colonists.

The introduced birds

The commonest birds on the largest and most species-rich island of Diego Garcia are the Madagascar Red Fody; Common Myna; Madagascar Turtle-dove; Zebra Dove; Cattle Egret and Red Junglefowl (Feral Chicken): all are introduced species. With the exception of the fody, which is found throughout BIOT, none of the other introduced species have sustained viable populations away from Diego Garcia and man. It is debateable, for example, whether chickens maintain their own populations away from Diego Garcia or whether in fact the outer atoll populations are actually supplemented by poachers as a food source for them. Common Myna was recorded on the Egmont Islands up to 1975; they now no longer appear present. House Sparrow has not been located on any of the atolls it thrived on when man was present and appears extinct in the Territory. Historically, a guineafowl species, Grey Francolin, and possibly a bulbul species were introduced and have all died out. It seems that in the harsh terrestrial environment of small oceanic islands that generally offer little food, introduced exotics do not fare well away from man. Cattle Egret has proven the exception to this observation. Successfully introduced onto Diego Garcia in the 1950s, the limiting factor now acting on this population is culling. The population has to be controlled due to bird strikes on aircraft. Even with this limitation, it is of interest that this species has spread and now breeds on two of the undisturbed islets in the mouth of the lagoon of Diego Garcia and appears regularly on Nelsons Island. It is likely that suitable habitat will limit the spread of Cattle Egret in BIOT: islands historically given over to coconut production that are now overgrown have little or no areas for these "open-space" birds to feed.

The seabirds

The archetypal avifauna of BIOT is its seabirds. These are now known to be present in globally important numbers. Up until 1971, there were 22 species of seabirds recorded as occurring and 14 of these were proven or strongly suspected of breeding (all of which have since been proven to breed). In 1996, the breeding species increased to 17 after the first comprehensive seabird survey. The first of the post 1971 new breeding species is Masked Booby, this, the rarest Sulidae (tropical gannets) regularly occurring in BIOT, has been found breeding on the two exposed rocky outcrops of Coin de Mire in Peros Banhos and Resurgent on the west-side of the Great Chagos Bank. The other new breeding species discovered post 1971 are Roseate and Little Tern. The eighteenth breeding seabird species was added when Red-tailed Tropicbird was found nesting on the edge of the sports field on Diego Garcia. It is unlikely this figure will increase in the near future. These four new breeding species nest in isolated locations at very low densities. This leads to the premise that the increase in number of breeding species is due to greater recording effort rather than a genuine influx of breeding birds.

There is evidence that at least Red-footed Booby is increasing in both numbers and range – this is likely to be due to the reduction of anthropogenic interference. Commander John Topp, Royal Navy, states of the Diego Garcia population, "When I was British Representative 1984–86 there was but a handful of Red-footed Boobies at Barton Point." Barton Point was made a restricted area during Cdr Topp's tenure and in May 2005, there were 4,370 breeding pairs there. Similarly, in 1996, Red-footed Booby was not found breeding in the Salomon Islands. In 2006, 323 pairs were breeding on two islands; by 2009, this had increased to four islands. It is likely that this species is colonising areas where it once bred now that man has vacated.

Of the non-breeding seabirds, by 1971, 22 species were reported as having definitely occurred; by 2009 this figure had increased to 35 (excluding Tropical Shearwater and Saunders' Tern). This increase is presumed to be a result of greater recording effort, better optical equipment and the quality of field-guides available rather than a genuine increase in the number of seabird species present or passing through.

The landbirds

In general terms, due to its isolation and relative young geological age, BIOT has an impoverished land bird community. Again, due to its remoteness and through a lack of permanent or extensive wetlands, estuaries or mudflats, BIOT does not support large numbers of associated birds, e.g. ducks, geese, storks, herons and waders. Dr Bill Bourne, in 1971, speculated of BIOT that "…it seems possible that there was once quite a rich landbird community, comparable to that of Christmas Island further east." This is certainly not true of the present avifauna.

Landbirds – the natural colonists: The three landbirds that are successful natural colonists are Striated Heron, White-breasted Waterhen and Common Moorhen. The heron has likely been on all of the atolls for centuries; the latter two are recent colonists to Diego Garcia. The first confirmed sighting of the waterhen was in 1995 and the Common Moorhen in 2007. Both species now breed continuously on Diego Garcia with the waterhen population in 2010 being estimated at 75–100 pairs and the moorhen at 10–15 pairs.

Of interest is the question of what will become of the "potential" colonists that are present on Diego Garcia in numbers that are sufficient to commence breeding? Yellow Bittern was first recorded on Diego Garcia in March 2004, when a small number of individuals were recorded from all around the island. Very small numbers of this species appear to be spending the northern hemisphere winter on Diego Garcia, though it may be possible that a tiny breeding population has been established. Similar circumstances surround the Indian Pond-heron on Diego Garcia; most likely another northern hemisphere winter visitor, though it is possible that the juvenile birds are of local stock. Great Egret and Little Egret have all historically occurred and in 2009 were still present in numbers of at least two. The fate of the three Black-crowned Night-heron found in November 2007 is uncertain, though the sighting of a further juvenile and an adult in March 2009 and further sightings of both juveniles and adults in October of the same year and again in October 2010, suggests it is a regular visitor in tiny numbers. The habitat on Diego Garcia is capable of sustaining populations of all these species but, as of yet there is no definite evidence of breeding. It is possible that there is some population size critical mass required, currently missing, to trigger breeding in these (mainly) colonial nesting species.

Landbirds – the migrants and vagrants: As Dr Bourne noted in 1971 of the atolls of BIOT, "They are isolated in the remotest possible position in the tropical Indian Ocean, in a situation lying in the path of landbird vagrants from three directions, the east, north and west…." Recent intense recording on Diego Garcia has shown that Dr Bourne was correct and that vagrants do occur, generally arriving from the north. For example, during an intense period of birdwatching in November 2007, 15 new species of birds for BIOT were found on Diego Garcia.

With the build up in ornithological knowledge of the area, it has been possible to assess which species are vagrants and which are regular migrants (albeit that they occur in small numbers). Certainly, the majority of the waders appear to be annual. Some such as Whimbrel, Ruddy Turnstone and Curlew Sandpiper turn up all across BIOT in their hundreds, if not in their very low thousands. Other species such as Sanderling, Bar-tailed Godwit, Common Greenshank, Wood and Common Sandpiper also appear to turn up annually on any of the atolls but in much smaller numbers. It is still unknown whether the final group of waders, those with very few records, such as Common Ringed Plover, Marsh Sandpiper and Common Redshank are annual visitors in extremely low numbers or merely occasional overshooting migrants.

Of the non-waders, Garganey appears annually, at least on Diego Garcia, as does Oriental Pratincole. The records of the remaining northern hemisphere birds are too few to be able to make a valued judgement upon the true status of the species, except to say that, to date, these species appear as vagrants.

The final species that warrants attention is House Crow, a species originally from the Indian Subcontinent but which has colonised many coastal areas around the fringe of the Indian Ocean, including some islands, and has even established populations in Europe. It readily travels by ship and initial colonisation of new areas generally seems to commence near busy ports. This pest species was first recorded in BIOT when a single bird was found present on Diego Garcia from at least May 2002. This, or another bird, was joined by a second in at least October 2008. The long-term fate of these two birds has yet to be revealed. It is noteworthy that the only known arrivals of pairs of House Crows that have *failed* to breed have been in southern Chile, where the pair died during their first boreal winter, in Australia where they were quickly trapped and shot and the Seychelles, where the founder population was shot and subsequent arrivals have been eradicated.

The British Government has placed this species on the BIOT pest list allowing it to be shot and trapped, though this has not been successful to date. Therefore, whether the two on Diego Garcia are male and female and, whether they will breed before being eradicated remains to be seen. The fact is, Diego Garcia is an ideal habitat for colonisation and for reasons of human health and seabird preservation, House Crow would be a most unwelcome addition to the avifauna.

Choice of 50 species

During late October to early April, with the aid of transport it is possible to see up to 50 species of bird on Diego Garcia. All of the common, introduced species can be found down town and, bizarrely, so can most of the seabirds. The two shearwaters can both be found year round in the centre of the built up area and most of the other seabirds can be viewed from an ocean-side beach. To see all of the waders a visit to the south of the island and some rough terrain walking with a telescope around the barachois is required. Of the 50 species illustrated, Masked Booby has never been recorded from Diego Garcia and is only regularly found on two islands of the outer atolls.

Bird names and order

The common and scientific names used throughout this book follow BirdLife International (2008), the BirdLife checklist of the birds of the world, with conservation status and taxonomic sources version 1, that can be downloaded from http://www.birdlife.org/datazone/species/downloads/BirdLife_Checklist_Version_1.zip [.xls zipped 1 MB].

Photographs

Where practical due to quality of photographs and, for authenticity of records, all photographs accompanying the following text are of birds photographed in BIOT, including firsts for the Territory and extreme rarities. Birds that were not photographed in the Territory have an asterisk * next to the photographer's acknowledgement.

Status and distribution

This section will give details of when and where the bird is likely to occur, including the preferred habitat where known. Also if the species breeds in BIOT, it will cover the islands that are used, with the preferred nesting habitat and the months when breeding is known to occur. There is still much to be learnt about status and distribution of both breeding and migratory birds in BIOT and everyone is encouraged to submit their records from the area to **www.worldbirds.org**.

Identification guide

This section is intended to guide a novice birdwatcher towards the species they are likely to be viewing in BIOT. It is not intended to be a comprehensive field guide (a guide to bird books that are useful in relation to

BIOT is found in the bibliography). When needed, it gives an indication of the size of the bird by comparing it to a familiar species. It then describes the key identification features used to identify birds that occur in BIOT. It should be noted that several species of migrants (mostly waders) that occur in BIOT are normally in non-breeding plumage and so this is the plumage described and is depicted in the accompanying picture.

Similar species
If there are similar species occurring in BIOT, they will be noted and the critical differences required for identification will be highlighted.

Local notes
This section gives details of any BIOT specific information for the species.

Other birds
In addition to the 50 species covered in depth, all other species that have been recorded in BIOT have their status and distribution briefly summarised. All of these records can also be viewed at **www.worldbirds.org**.

Chris Patrick

Red Junglefowl (Domestic Chicken) *Gallus gallus* (Linnaeus, 1758)

STATUS AND DISTRIBUTION: Breeding resident, broods of chicks being found throughout the year. On rat-infested Diego Garcia there is a healthy population of over 100 birds that do not restrict themselves to areas of human habitation. The status and distribution of these once domestic chickens throughout the remainder of BIOT is not fully known; limited evidence suggests that where they were once kept as food on large islands they are still extant (e.g. Eagle Island and Ile Sudest, Egmont Islands). Elsewhere, chickens are present on at least: Nelsons Island, Sea Cow, South Brother and Danger Island (all atolls that were never inhabited).

IDENTIFICATION GUIDE: Unmistakeable. Of interest, on Diego Garcia, a black and silver plumage is the most predominant, whilst on the outer islands a golden and tan variety is the most numerous.

LOCAL NOTES: Chickens are thought to have been released by poachers on the islands that have never been inhabited as a food source when operating out of illegal poaching camps. The outer island populations still have the ability to fly for short distances.

Chris Patrick

Cattle Egret *Bubulcus ibis* (Linnaeus, 1758)

STATUS AND DISTRIBUTION: Breeding resident. This species has a relatively well documented history in the Chagos. Cattle Egret were appearing as vagrants in the area as far back as 1885, one being collected by G.C. Bourne on Diego Garcia of the subspecies *coromandas* in September of that year. In the 1950s, Cattle Egret were deliberately introduced to Diego Garcia from the Seychelles with birds being released to control arthropods. In December 1960, 27 nests belonging to their descendants were recorded at East Point. In the 1990s, Cattle Egret were at their highest population density in the mid-90s, with a single flock of 248 at the landfill site in 1995. By 2002, breeding had switched from East Point to Point Marianne. Due to culling, numbers dropped considerably thereafter with only a maximum of 50 birds being seen on any day in December 2002. In 2005, numbers remained low with a maximum of 30–50 birds being recorded in May, with six pairs breeding on West Island and the Point Marianne site deserted. These easily accessible nests on West Island exposed a spread of laying and hatching dates. In November 2007, breeding was recorded again on West Island with 20–25 pairs and a new rookery on East Island that held six pairs. The total population in November 2007 was estimated at 150–200 birds. In 2008, breeding was still occurring throughout the year in both of the rookeries located in 2007. In 2010, the resident population is estimated to be in the region of 350 birds on Diego Garcia. Other records between October 2008 and October 2010 exist, recording this species from the Salomon Islands, Egmont Islands and islands of the Great Chagos Bank: the highest count being eight birds on Nelsons Island in November 2008.

IDENTIFICATION GUIDE: Exceptionally tame and extremely numerous, particularly around habitation on Diego Garcia, generally any white "heron-looking" bird will be this species. Birds in breeding plumage have coral-red legs and bill and golden streaks on their backs and breast. Non-breeders are all white with greeny-black legs and a yellow bill.

SIMILAR SPECIES: Both Little and Dimorphic Egret have been recorded on Diego Garcia and superficially resemble Cattle Egret. Both of these rarities have black bills (Cattle Egret is yellow) and yellow feet and are slimmer looking and taller.

LOCAL NOTES: This species is particularly numerous at the landfill site where grubby looking birds forage amongst the rubbish. It is controlled on Diego Garcia in order to minimise the possibility of aircraft strikes from the numerous birds that congregate to feed and loaf on the airfield.

Chris Patrick

Madagascar Turtle-dove *Nesoenas picturata* Temminck, 1813

Janet Prushansky

STATUS AND DISTRIBUTION: Breeding resident: it is presumed (from displaying and calling birds) that this species breeds throughout the year. It is found only on Diego Garcia and the population is estimated to be in the region of 100–200 breeding pairs.

IDENTIFICATION GUIDE: Unmistakeable, the only large brown pigeon to be found in BIOT.

LOCAL NOTES: It is a mystery why this species is not found on the other atolls where plantations once existed, as it was extremely likely to have been kept for food and therefore would have escaped; as presumably happened on Diego Garcia. The mystery is compounded further by the fact that birds are equally as common in Downtown Diego Garcia as they are in the uninhabited wilder eastern arm of the island.

Chris Patrick

Zebra Dove *Geopelia striata* (Linnaeus, 1766)

Janet Prushansky

STATUS AND DISTRIBUTION: Breeding resident: it is presumed (from displaying and calling birds) that this species breeds throughout the year. This species is confined to Diego Garcia and the population in 2010 is estimated at 100–200 breeding pairs.

IDENTIFICATION GUIDE: Very tame and unmistakeable, the only small tan coloured dove in BIOT. When perched on fences it can appear very cuckoo-like: the blue facial skin is always diagnostic.

LOCAL NOTES: This species was introduced from the Seychelles in 1960 and is equally numerous on both the Downtown and uninhabited arm of the island.

Chris Patrick

Common Myna *Acridotheres tristis* (Linnaeus, 1766)

STATUS AND DISTRIBUTION: Breeding resident. The presence of duller coloured, food-begging juveniles with brighter coloured adults during November and December strongly indicates a breeding season between October and January. This species is confined to Diego Garcia, though was once found on at least the Egmont Islands. The population is estimated at between 500–1,000 birds in 2010.

IDENTIFICATION GUIDE: The size of a Starling, this bird is tame and unmistakeable, the only bird of its type to regularly occur in the area.

LOCAL NOTES: This species is affected by a feather mite, therefore miniature vulture-like, featherless, yellow- headed individuals are not uncommon.

Janet Prushansky

Birds communally roost in the Downtown area of Diego Garcia and these gatherings at dusk are very noisy and continue for some time after the sun has gone down.

Chris Patrick

Madagascar Red Fody *Foudia madagascariensis* (Linnaeus, 1766)

STATUS AND DISTRIBUTION: Breeding resident on all BIOT atolls. Breeding males assume their brilliant red breeding plumage from September and there are large numbers of juveniles in October and November; indicating a breeding season from September to December. On Diego Garcia, the woven nests have been found in shrubs adjoining the airfield. This species was first noted on Diego Garcia in 1884, though the exact date of introduction is not known. The current population on Diego Garcia is estimated at between 500–1,000 individuals. Madagascar Red Fody is the only passerine regularly found throughout all of BIOT, occurring on every atoll that is large enough to support sufficient vegetation for it to breed and feed in.

IDENTIFICATION GUIDE: The size of a sparrow, it is tame and unmistakeable even in non-breeding plumage; it is the only "finch-like" bird to occur in the area.

LOCAL NOTES: Very common in Downtown Diego Garcia where it will even enter accommodation in search of food. Large gatherings of up to a hundred individuals can occur at sites where birds are regularly fed.

Other introduced birds

House Sparrow *Passer domesticus* (Linnaeus, 1758)

By 1905 this species had been introduced to Peros Banhos and the Salomon Islands where it was still present and common in 1960. Despite extensive searches between 2008 and 2010, no House Sparrow was found on any atoll and it is possible that this commensal of man has died out in BIOT.

Janet Prushansky *

SEABIRDS

Andy Williams

Wedge-tailed Shearwater *Puffinus pacificus* (Gmelin, 1789)

STATUS AND DISTRIBUTION: Breeding resident. This, the commonest of the three regularly occurring shearwater species, has been recorded extensively from the seas of the Chagos including, in small numbers, offshore from Diego Garcia. Historically, it has bred between November and March on the Great Chagos Bank islands of North Brother, Sea Cow, South Brother, Resurgent, Nelsons Island and from Peros Banhos on Yéyé, Grand Coquillage and Coin de Mire. A census in 2006 gave a total breeding population of 2,683 pairs, distributed between North Brother (1,581 pairs); Sea Cow (719 pairs) and South Brother (563 pairs): this census did not visit Nelsons Island and found no shearwaters breeding in the Peros Banhos group. In 2010, a census in February revealed 2,411 breeding pairs distributed between North Brother (2,000), Sea Cow (110), South Brother (300) and Coin de Mire, Peros Banhos (1). In addition to the above breeding records and of interest, on rat-infested Diego Garcia, there is a small breeding population (1–5 pairs) scattered in the Downtown area that nests under vegetation (mainly Screw Pine *Pandanus utilus*) throughout the year. This part of Diego Garcia could be suitable for breeding because the rats are heavily controlled in this area. At sea, this is the most common shearwater and appears most numerous between October and March. It is regularly recorded during sea-watches off Diego Garcia.

IDENTIFICATION GUIDE: Two pale-phase Wedge-tailed Shearwaters have been recorded from BIOT waters but all of the regular breeding population appear to be dark-phase birds. It is a slim looking chocolate-brown bird with a distinctive long wedge-shaped tail and it flies in typical shearwater fashion, skimming low over wave tops.

SIMILAR SPECIES: The only other species likely to be encountered in BIOT waters that may present confusion is Flesh-footed Shearwater. Look for that species' broader wings and fleshy-pink feet and straw-coloured bill, the latter being evident at long distance.

LOCAL NOTES: Watch for this species as they glide in silently to their nests in Downtown Diego Garcia as night falls. They clumsily land on the manicured grass and stumble away until safely under their chosen shrub; outside the BIOT Police HQ is a good spot. Their nesting areas on Diego Garcia are known as "cat-bushes" due to the mewing call the chicks make from them as darkness falls.

Ian Lewis*

Flesh-footed Shearwater *Puffinus carneipes* Gould, 1844

STATUS AND DISTRIBUTION: Non-breeding visitor. There are records of definite sightings of this species in BIOT waters in the months of February, March, April, May, July and October. On Diego Garcia, three birds were recorded passing Simpson Point in strong south-easterly winds on 05 November 2007 and again on 14 November 2009 during strong westerly onshore winds

IDENTIFICATION GUIDE: This is the largest of the three shearwaters that regularly occurs in BIOT waters. With an all-dark body and broad wings, the pale horn bill with dark tip when combined with pink feet is diagnostic.

SIMILAR SPECIES: See Wedge-tailed Shearwater. This species looks languid in flight and once this lazy looking flight pattern is known, this species can be identified at range.

LOCAL NOTES: It is the rarest of the three regularly occurring shearwaters.

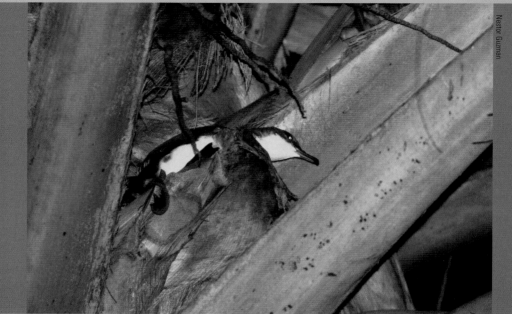

Nestor Guzman

Audubon's Shearwater *Puffinus lherminieri* Lesson, 1839
including **Tropical Shearwater** *Puffinus bailloni* (Bonaparte, 1857)

STATUS AND DISTRIBUTION: Breeding resident. Not as numerous as Wedge-tailed Shearwater, this species is found throughout BIOT waters in small numbers in all months, including offshore from Diego Garcia. It has been recorded as breeding between December and March on North Brother (420 pairs in 1996, 183 pairs in 2006, 166 pairs in 2010); South Brother (150 pairs in 1996) and Coin de Mire (12 pairs in 1996). It has recently been found breeding on Petite Coquillage in Peros Banhos (5–10 pairs in 2009). It was found and photographed in the Downtown area of Diego Garcia in 2004 and is suspected of breeding on Diego Garcia with its wailing call being regularly heard in the Downtown area between October 2008 and October 2010.

Nestor Guzman

IDENTIFICATION GUIDE: This is the only shearwater of this complex group thought to occur in BIOT waters regularly. Its smaller size, faster wing beats and more "auk-like" impression when viewed at range readily distinguish it from the two other larger, all-dark, longer-winged shearwaters that occur.

LOCAL NOTES: This complex species group has recently been reviewed and the species found in BIOT is Tropical Shearwater *Puffinus bailloni* (Bonaparte, 1857); most, if not all, historical records of Audubon's Shearwater are likely to refer to Tropical Shearwater.

Glen Tepke (pbase.com/gtepke)*

Wilson's Storm-petrel *Oceanites oceanicus* (Kuhl, 1820)

STATUS AND DISTRIBUTION: Rare non-breeding visitor. There are numerous historic records of this species at sea in BIOT waters from all months: the latest record being a photographed bird off North Brother on 01 June 2010. There is a single record from Diego Garcia of two birds passing Eclipse Point on 31 May 2005.

IDENTIFICATION GUIDE: The only bird of its size and shape likely to be encountered in BIOT waters, its tiny size, distinctive flight and white crescent across the rump make this an easy seabird to identify.

SIMILAR SPECIES: The other petrels and Storm-petrels that have occurred in BIOT waters that could potentially be misidentified as Wilson's are all desperately rare. All other potential misidentifications species do not have a white rump and/or have white on their undersides.

LOCAL NOTES: This species is attracted to the bright lights of ships and has been known to land onboard vessels in BIOT waters and remain on them overnight.

Jean Evans*

Red-tailed Tropicbird *Phaethon rubricauda* Boddaert, 1783

STATUS AND DISTRIBUTION: An uncommon breeding resident and an enigmatic species in BIOT. There are historic records from all of the atolls in the Chagos, though to date it has only been proven to breed on Diego Garcia. One pair was found breeding on Diego Garcia in 1996, in a bizarre choice of nesting site: in shrubs some 10 metres behind the soccer goal in the sports recreation area. The highest annual breeding numbers peaked at 16 pairs in 2002. Records show that this species breeds all year round on Diego Garcia with the peak nesting period being between December and March. This colony has been impacted by an infestation of dodder *Cassytha filiformis* L. smothering the breeding area. However, at least 2–5 pairs were still breeding there in March 2009. It is likely that this species breeds in very small numbers on other atolls of the Chagos.

IDENTIFICATION GUIDE: This species' coral-red bill and tail streamers easily identify adults in breeding plumage. Adults lacking tail streamers have minimal but distinctive black markings on their upper-wings and retain the red bill. Juveniles, lacking the red bill and long tail, have barred upperparts and a dark-yellow bill.

SIMILAR SPECIES: See White-tailed Tropicbird. Adults are easily separable on tail colour and diagnostic upper-wing patterns and are much larger than White-tailed Tropicbird. Juveniles can be problematic. With good views the darker wing tips of White-tailed are the key to identification.

LOCAL NOTES: Look for this species on Diego Garcia coming in to land on the soccer pitch and hopping away to its nest under the vegetation behind the soccer goal furthest away from the road.

Chris Patrick

White-tailed Tropicbird *Phaethon lepturus* Daudin, 1802

STATUS AND DISTRIBUTION: Breeding resident. Although by no means numerous, this species is the commonest of the Phaethontidae to occur in the Chagos and is regularly seen around all of the atolls. It has been recorded as breeding on Diego Garcia as far back as the start of the 1900s, in 1996 breeding was recorded during February and March from Diego Garcia (3 pairs), Peros Banhos (5 pairs) and Salomon Islands (5 pairs). In 2006, seven breeding pairs were located; one pair on Diego Garcia; the remaining pairs in the Salomon Islands. Non-breeding birds are a fairly regular sight over Diego Garcia, usually in small groups of 2–4 birds that are easily located by their constant and distinct flight call.

Janet Prushansky

The golden-washed subspecies *fulvus*

IDENTIFICATION GUIDE: This species' yellow bill, white tail feathers and distinctive wing pattern should distinguish it from Red-tailed Tropicbird: the only species found in BIOT waters it is likely to be confused with.

LOCAL NOTES: A beautiful golden-washed subspecies of White-tailed Tropicbird (ssp. *fulvus*) was thought to be endemic to Christmas Island, over a thousand miles away. This stunning looking bird has been seen and photographed in 2007 and again in 2009 on Diego Garcia; the most recent sighting being of a nest prospecting bird. It is possible that this subspecies is regular in BIOT and may even nest in very small numbers.

Pete Carr

Greater Frigatebird *Fregata minor* (Gmelin, 1789)

STATUS AND DISTRIBUTION: Common resident species with very local breeding. It is the more numerous of the two frigatebirds present in the Chagos and is found on all atolls. It is particularly numerous wherever there is an abundance of Red-footed Booby: the species it mainly pirates upon for regurgitated food as they return from fishing excursions. Whilst easily seen in the archipelago, it is restricted to very few islands as a breeding species. In January 1975, North Brother had an estimated 300 pairs at the egg laying stage. In 1996, during February and March, this island held 85 breeding pairs. In July 2009, North Brother had 300 pairs breeding, in addition to 50 pairs on Grand Coquillage, Peros Banhos – a new breeding island. In February 2010, there were 80 pairs breeding on North Brother, 5–10 pairs on Middle Brother, a new breeding site and 31 pairs breeding on Grand Coquillage. This species breeds continuously throughout the year. The Three Brothers hold the largest non-breeding roosts, regularly having 500–1,000 birds moving in to and departing the islands at dawn and dusk. Away from this stronghold, East Island in the mouth of Diego Garcia lagoon regularly supports roosts of up to 250 birds.

IDENTIFICATION GUIDE: Frigatebirds are very noticeable and can be identified when clear views are had of their undersides when flying. However, the two species that occur in BIOT, Greater and Lesser Frigatebird, can be a problem pair to distinguish between, due to both species having many different plumages related to age and sex. Adult males are all black. Generally, in this species the greater extent of grey / white on the chin, breast and belly and the lack of white spurs in the axillaries (arm-pits) of females and young are diagnostic. Perched frigatebirds are also problematical to identify and this may have caused confusion in the past about which islands the two local species nest on.

SIMILAR SPECIES: Lesser Frigatebird is the only other species that has occurred in BIOT waters with which it could be confused. Adult male Lesser Frigatebirds are all black except for white axillary patches. Careful viewing of the axillaries is the easiest feature to differentiate females and young; if the white in the arm-pit extends outwards from the belly, it is Lesser Frigatebird. The other diagnostic feature is the extent of white on the breast and belly: generally, in sub-adult birds, Greater Frigatebird has white that extends further down the belly.

Chris Patrick

LOCAL NOTES: The aerial skill of these birds as they parasitise Red-footed Boobies returning to islands with full crops is incredible. They chase the victim, nipping its wings and tail until the booby regurgitates its crop contents, which are then caught mid air before they hit the water. A good spot to watch this spectacle is the O Club on Diego Garcia in late afternoon as the boobies return to their nests or to roost on West Island. The courtship display of this species is also spectacular. The males stand on their nests and outstretch their wings, then inflate their fiery-red gular (throat) pouches and emit a far carrying and unearthly warbling "lululululu" call. It is the characteristic sight and call, which is long remembered after a visit to North Brother or Grand Coquillage.

Pete Carr

Lesser Frigatebird *Fregata ariel* (Gray, 1845)

Pete Carr

STATUS AND DISTRIBUTION: Common resident species with very local breeding. This species is widespread and found in all atolls, although not as numerous as Greater Frigatebird. It was first recorded as breeding in the Chagos Archipelago on Nelsons Island, when 250 pairs at the egg laying stage were found in January / February 1975. Nelsons Island remains the breeding stronghold for this species with 40 pairs breeding there in July 2009 and 50 pairs breeding in February 2010. It also breeds on North Brother where there were 12 pairs in 1996 and 10 pairs in 2010. There are records of Lesser Frigatebird breeding on two other islands, although these are thought to be erroneous and should refer to Greater Frigatebird. Gatherings of loafing non-breeding birds are regular on East Island, Diego Garcia, with a high count of 60 adults recorded in July 1995.

IDENTIFICATION GUIDE: See Greater Frigatebird. In all plumages the white spurs of the axillaries are diagnostic.

LOCAL NOTES: Similar to Greater Frigatebird, this species parasitises Red-footed Booby and is found throughout BIOT wherever its host is present in any numbers.

Pete Carr

Masked Booby *Sula dactylatra* Lesson, 1831

STATUS AND DISTRIBUTION: Local breeding resident. This species has been recorded fairly regularly and in good numbers at sea in the Chagos Archipelago, for example a flock of over 150 birds were feeding midway between Peros Banhos and the Salomon Islands on 14 November 2008. It has, however, only ever been recorded on land on the two bare rocky islands of Resurgent and Coin de Mire, Peros Banhos. The first breeding records are of some 190 pairs on Resurgent, which were at all stages of breeding between December 1974 and April 1975. In February and March 1996, 160 pairs were breeding on Resurgent and a further 85 pairs on Coin de Mire. In March 2006, there were 160 pairs breeding on Resurgent and 11 pairs on Coin de Mire. In November 2008, there were 60 incubating birds on Resurgent; in July 2009 there were 30 pairs breeding; in February 2010 there were 40 pairs breeding; and in June 2010, 140 pairs were breeding. On Coin de Mire, there were in the region of 10 pairs breeding continuously between December 2008 and June 2010. The peak breeding period for this species in BIOT, if there is one, is not known to date.

IDENTIFICATION GUIDE: A striking black and white booby. The pure white colouration and black mask combined with its restricted range in BIOT should identify all adults. Juveniles are much darker than adults and can resemble juvenile Brown Booby. Juvenile Masked Booby is a lighter brown, has a white collar and whiter underwings.

SIMILAR SPECIES: Adults can be mistaken for Red-footed Booby at a distance; this species never shows yellow in the head and is a much purer outstanding white. Juveniles superficially resemble Brown Booby, see under Identification Guide.

LOCAL NOTES: Masked Booby is seldom encountered in BIOT waters away from the two breeding colonies and has never been recorded from Diego Garcia.

Chris Patrick

Red-footed Booby *Sula sula* (Linnaeus, 1766)

STATUS AND DISTRIBUTION: Common breeding resident. This is the commonest *Sulidae* occurring in BIOT, found throughout the entire Territory. It appears to be expanding its range into areas that it most likely formerly bred in and has seemingly increased in numbers since at least 1970. It has (re)colonised the now uninhabited Salomon Islands since at least 1996, when this atoll was surveyed and no birds were found breeding; in November 2008, there were over 100 pairs breeding on Mapou and smaller numbers on Ile du Passe and Takamaka. It has also (re)colonised the Egmont Islands with at least 30 pairs breeding on Ile Carre Pate in February 2010. On Diego Garcia in 1971, it was only ever recorded on the lagoon islets; by 2010, there were an estimated 5,325 breeding pairs, nesting from Cust Point ocean-side to Shark's Cove lagoon-side. It has a very complicated breeding phenology, with differing breeding periods in the same colony as well as between islands and atolls. The peak breeding period appears to be between December and April, though breeding birds can be found on all atolls throughout the year.

IDENTIFICATION GUIDE: A beautiful bird in breeding plumage, the intensity of the colours of the feet and bill increase as peak breeding condition is reached. Adults are readily distinguishable by their black and white wings with a distinctive black patch at the bend of the wing on the underside and the diagnostic yellow on the head. Juveniles require more care in identifying them from the other two booby species: the all-brown body of juveniles of this species is diagnostic.

SIMILAR SPECIES: Adult Masked Booby can be confused with adult Red-footed Booby. The yellow wash on the head and the distinctive underwing pattern of the subspecies of Red-footed Booby occurring in BIOT should distinguish all. Immature birds could be mistaken for Abbott's Booby: this extreme rarity always has a black tail. The all-brown body of juveniles differentiates this species from both juvenile Brown and Masked Booby.

LOCAL NOTES: It is the only booby regularly encountered on Diego Garcia and hundreds can be observed in the early evening passing the Downtown area, returning to the islets in the mouth of the lagoon to roost. Over 99.9% of the birds occurring in BIOT are of the wholly white morph; though there are two records of two white-tailed brown morph birds; one on Diego Garcia in 1995 and in November 2008, and again in November 2009, in the same nest, a brown morph adult was found incubating on Petite Coquillage, Peros Banhos.

Chris Patrick

Brown Booby *Sula leucogaster* (Boddaert, 1783)

STATUS AND DISTRIBUTION: Fairly common resident and localised breeding species. Small numbers of non-breeding birds can be found at any time of the year on all atolls. This species breeds throughout the year in BIOT with no discernible peak period. The stronghold for the species is North Brother with 685 pairs breeding in March 2006, 650 breeding pairs in July 2009 and 600 pairs in February 2010. Danger Island has the second largest breeding concentration with 245 breeding pairs in March 1996, 60 pairs in April 2009 and 80 pairs in May 2010. Other smaller breeding populations exist on Nelsons Island and in amongst the Masked Booby on the two rocky outcrops of Resurgent and Coin de Mire. It is recorded regularly on the three islets in the mouth of the lagoon of Diego Garcia and roosts of up to 25 birds have been found at Barton Point on mainland Diego Garcia.

IDENTIFICATION GUIDE: The chocolate-brown upperparts and head coupled with the pure white belly and central panel of the underwings make the adults very distinctive. Juveniles look like faded adults, the upperparts are a duller brown and the white of the under parts appear smudged with brown.

SIMILAR SPECIES: Only juvenile Masked Booby could be mistaken for this species in BIOT waters. Masked Booby juveniles are noticeably paler brown and have a white cervical collar that can be seen at good ranges at sea.

LOCAL NOTES: This species always nests on the ground in open areas with no or very low vegetation, generally with a direct flight path to the ocean. When commencing breeding it decorates its nest with fresh vegetation. Unlike Red-footed Booby, it will occasionally lay two eggs, though it seldomly raises two chicks to fledging successfully.

Janet Prushansky

Great Crested Tern *Sterna bergii* Lichtenstein, 1823

STATUS AND DISTRIBUTION: Common resident and nomadic breeding species. This is a fairly common species throughout BIOT and breeds in small (up to 40 pairs) isolated colonies in no fixed months, though the peak numbers period appears to be between December and April. It does not have established breeding colonies on specific islands in BIOT: it nests randomly on sandy beaches or sand spits throughout all of the atolls. The long sand bar that extends between the two halves of the Egmont Islands appears to be a preferred nesting area with 40 pairs breeding on it in February 2009 and 15 pairs breeding there again in July 2009. It can nest on rat-infested islands and it has been recorded as breeding on Diego Garcia where it is a common sight all around the shoreline of the lagoon.

IDENTIFICATION GUIDE: It is the by far the largest tern that regularly occurs in BIOT and is therefore unmistakeable. Its scruffy crest and prominent yellow bill are very noticeable when roosting.

SIMILAR SPECIES: The Lesser Crested Tern has been recorded in BIOT, though is extremely rare: it is slightly smaller, has a smarter looking black cap and a diagnostic orange bill.

LOCAL NOTES: High tide mixed tern roosts at Point Marianne on Diego Garcia can hold over 50 Great Crested Tern. Juveniles remain with the parents for weeks after fledging and are often seen and heard begging for food from them.

Nigel Phillips

Common Tern *Sterna hirundo* Linnaeus, 1758

STATUS AND DISTRIBUTION: A very rare but probable annual non-breeding visitor to BIOT. The first record of this species in BIOT comes from 1972–73 in the Egmont Islands. There is a record from Middle Brother in March 1975 (the only other record away from Diego Garcia). There are several records of this species on Diego Garcia back to 1995, all indicating that this species is chiefly a northern hemisphere winter visitor in very small numbers. The few birds that do occur, stay for lengthy periods and are generally found on the Downtown sewage farm settling ponds, arriving in November and departing by early May the following year.

IDENTIFICATION GUIDE: Easily identified as a typical sea tern, in breeding plumage the black-tipped blood-red bill and when in flight, the extent of black on the outer underwing are diagnostic. In non-breeding plumage the bill is black and the forehead becomes a white patch. Birds in juvenile plumage have not been recorded, though second summer birds that retain a vestige of a wing bar have been noted.

SIMILAR SPECIES: Both Arctic and White-cheeked Tern occur in BIOT and superficially resemble Common Tern, this is particularly so in non-breeding plumage. White-cheeked Tern has a grey rump and tail, much less black on the outer underwing and greyer upper-wings. In all plumages, White-cheeked behaves much more like a freshwater marsh tern, in that it hovers and dip-feeds over freshwater areas. Arctic Tern in non-breeding plumage can be problematical unless viewed well when the cleaner underwing pattern proves diagnostic.

LOCAL NOTES: Common Tern is most easily found on Diego Garcia roosting on the wires that stretch over the settling ponds of the Downtown sewage works. To assist with identification, it is usually found amongst at least White-winged Terns and occasionally White-cheeked Terns to which it can be compared.

Richard Jeanne*

Roseate Tern *Sterna dougallii* Montagu, 1813

STATUS AND DISTRIBUTION: Rare resident and extremely rare and localised breeding species. Not a common species in BIOT, the largest day counts being of c.15 birds on Diego Garcia on three days in April 1971. It has been proven to breed in very small numbers (less than 5 pairs) on Diego Garcia, Peros Banhos and the Salomon Islands and probably breeds on the sand bar between the Egmont Islands too. Coin de Mire, Peros Banhos is the most dependable breeding location. To date, breeding has only been recorded between December and April. It is most numerous during the northern hemisphere winter, though some individual birds are present throughout the year.

IDENTIFICATION GUIDE: The pink hue of the breast and purer white plumage make Roseate Tern unmistakeable in summer plumage. Adults out of summer plumage are more usually found in BIOT and are fairly distinctive by their red legs, black bill and attenuated look due to the long tail feathers. Fortunately, there are no other terns that look like Roseate Tern in juvenile or first winter plumage, terefore black-legged, black-billed birds with brown-scaled plumages are highly likely to be this species.

SIMILAR SPECIES: First summer birds can resemble Common Tern of a similar age. Roseate Tern is always paler and looks longer winged.

LOCAL NOTES: On Diego Garcia look for this species roosting on the derelict pier at East Point Plantation amongst the more common Crested and Black-naped Terns.

Pete Carr

Black-naped Tern *Sterna sumatrana* Raffles, 1822

STATUS AND DISTRIBUTION: Common resident and nomadic breeding species. Probably the most abundant of the true Sternidae terns occurring in BIOT, loafing flocks of 30–40 birds can be encountered on isolated sand bars on any atoll throughout the year. An apparently nomadic breeding species, it has been recorded nesting on every atoll, though does not appear to consistently nest on the same islands within atolls year after year. The preferred nesting habitat is open sandy or stony shorelines and colony size ranges from 5–40 pairs. The main breeding period is between November and May.

Pete Carr

IDENTIFICATION GUIDE: With decent views, the pure white adults with black head-bands are unlikely to be confused with any other species in BIOT. Juveniles are unlikely to be confused as they are brown-scaled with brown-grey crowns and are always invariably accompanied by adults.

SIMILAR SPECIES: In BIOT, the only similar species would be a juvenile of the extremely rare breeding Roseate Tern, which could possibly be mistaken for a juvenile Black-naped Tern. Juvenile Roseate Tern has a much darker crown and bill.

LOCAL NOTES: Look for this species around the Marina on Diego Garcia or, if access is allowed, breeding on the roof of the building at the end of POL Pier. It has been recorded as breeding on the ground on rat-infested islands in BIOT.

Janet Prushansky

Little Tern *Sterna albifrons* Pallas, 1764
including **Saunders's Tern** *Sterna saundersi* Hume, 1877

STATUS AND DISTRIBUTION: The true status of *Sterna albifrons* and *S. saundersi* in BIOT remains uncertain due to the identification challenge of non-breeding and juvenile birds. "Little Terns" are not uncommon in BIOT, particularly on Diego Garcia, where, for example, a total of 159 birds were recorded on 01 November 2007; these were all claimed as *albifrons*. The first indication of breeding comes from two recently fledged birds on Diego Garcia on 29 July 1995 and further breeding pairs of definite *albifrons* were found again on Diego Garcia in March 1996 and February 2006. There have been numerous claims of Saunders's Tern, though none have been supported by enough evidence to verify the claim. As this species is thought to be indistinguishable from *S. albifrons* in all but adult summer plumage, all records of *S. saundersi* must be treated as circumspect. It is likely that the true situation is that Little Tern breeds in tiny numbers (1–10 pairs), centred upon a population on Diego Garcia, though limited breeding may take place on other atolls. These breeding birds are supplemented between October and April by migrant birds. Saunders's Tern may turn up in BIOT as a vagrant with the wintering Little Terns and due to identification challenges they will go unrecorded.

IDENTIFICATION GUIDE: Certain identification can only be made when clear views of adults in breeding plumage are had. Harrison's Seabirds states that Saunders's Tern has darker wingtips, a greyer rump and back and lacks the white superciliary over the eye.

LOCAL NOTES: The sand bank that often holds a mixed tern roost at high-tide at Point Marianne, accessible through Thunder Cove, is the most reliable site on Diego Garcia for this species and is where the largest roosts of Little Terns are found.

Derrick Wilby

Bridled Tern *Sterna anaethetus* Scopoli, 1786

STATUS AND DISTRIBUTION: A rare resident and localised breeding species. Whilst it has likely always been resident in small numbers in BIOT, the first published record ever was of three birds on the Egmont Isles on 31 December 1972. It has since then been recorded in low numbers from all atolls, in all months. It has been proven to breed on the Great Chagos Bank islands of Sea Cow; North Brother; Resurgent; South Brother and Nelsons Island and also on West Island (Diego Garcia) and on Coin du Mire and Parasol (Peros Banhos). It is likely to be found breeding in low densities on other islands, particularly those that have remained rat-free. Nelsons Island has had the largest breeding total with 17 pairs in February 1973; North Brother is the other stronghold, holding 15 breeding pairs in March 1996. It has been recorded as breeding throughout the year, with birds laying asynchronously on the same island. In BIOT, this species tends to nest in stone crevices and cracks in rocks along the shoreline.

IDENTIFICATION GUIDE: With good views, this is not a difficult bird to identify. It is a warm chocolate-brown colour on the upperparts and has less white than Sooty Tern on the forehead that extends in a thin line back over the eye. The call is very distinctive and given all the time in flight when their nests are approached: it is a much less raucous sound than Sooty Tern.

SIMILAR SPECIES: Sooty Tern is potentially the only species in BIOT it could be confused with. Sooty Tern is much darker on the upperparts, lacks the pale collar, has a much harsher ear-splitting call and generally is seen in BIOT in far greater numbers. Bridled Terns are seldom found in numbers greater than 10 anywhere in the Territory.

LOCAL NOTES: Sailing past Coin du Mire is possibly the most reliable way to see this species in BIOT. It has been recorded on sea watches from Diego Garcia, particularly when strong onshore winds are blowing.

Andy Williams

Sooty Tern *Sterna fuscata* Linnaeus, 1766

STATUS AND DISTRIBUTION: Not a common species throughout the Territory, except on islands where it breeds in dense colonies. Sooty Tern has been impacted catastrophically as a breeding species by the presence of man and his commensals, particularly on Diego Garcia. For example, the breeding population on Diego Garcia was estimated in the order of 100,000 pairs in July 1884 and shortly after was thought to have completely ceased breeding on this atoll. Since 1996, breeding has been recorded on Danger Island, Sea Cow, the Three Brothers, and, in Peros Banhos, Parasol, Longue, Petite and Grand Coquillage and Petie Ile Bois Mangue. In February 1996, 73,000 breeding pairs were found throughout the Territory; in 2006, a total of 82,208 pairs were found. The breeding phenology of this species in BIOT is not understood. It has been recorded breeding throughout the year and does not nest on all islands where it is known to breed in any given year. Therefore, an accurate figure for the total breeding population in the Territory cannot yet be given. Away from the breeding islands, it is only occasionally seen and is by no means common. On Diego Garcia, it is more often heard flying over at night calling than seen off the shore.

IDENTIFICATION GUIDE: With good views, adults should not be confused with the other dark and white tern in BIOT, Bridled Tern being a warm brown colour whilst Sooty Tern is a sooty-black colour. Juveniles are separable on general colour, young Bridled Terns are much lighter coloured and have paler crowns, while juvenile Sooty Terns are dull sooty-black above and below with variable white or beige spots on the upperparts. Juveniles of these species are unlikely to be encountered on the same islands and Bridled is seldom found far away from land. The most likely area where the two species will be seen together is around Resurgent, where a small number of breeding Bridled Tern are sandwiched between Sooty Tern colonies on South and Middle Brother.

LOCAL NOTES: This species is particularly attracted to the lights of ships at night and hundreds have been known to continuously circle lighted ships raucously calling and often landing on the decks in large numbers.

Chris Patrick

White-winged Tern *Chlidonias leucopterus* (Temminck, 1815)

STATUS AND DISTRIBUTION: A rare but regular northern hemisphere winter visitor. Which marsh tern occurs in BIOT was something of a mystery until recent years, there having been various unconfirmed records of all three *Chlidonias* species. With the advent of quality field guides and digital photography, it has been revealed that it is this species that spends the northern hemisphere winter on the freshwater sewage ponds of Diego Garcia and likely sporadically occurs elsewhere, especially on passage. The first birds arrive in October and have usually departed by the first week of April; there is one exceptional record of two birds on Diego Garcia on 28 May 2005. In March 1997, 19 marsh terns were on Diego Garcia, though were not specifically identified. The highest confirmed total is 12 birds present between 04–06 November 2009.

IDENTIFICATION NOTES: Occasionally birds arrive in the Territory with vestiges of black underwings and prior to returning to their breeding grounds some birds start moulting in to the stunning black and white breeding plumage; these birds are easy to identify. Most birds reaching BIOT are already in winter plumage. Careful observation of the overall pattern and amount of dark colouring on the head, lack of dark patches on the sides of breast and the obvious white rump are all indicative of this species.

SIMILAR SPECIES: There is a single unconfirmed record of Black Tern *Chlidonias niger* in the Egmont Islands from 1975 and a single unconfirmed record of Whiskered Tern *Chlidonia hybridus* from Diego Garcia in 1995; both superficially resemble White-winged Tern in juvenile and winter plumage. It is unlikely a bird in full breeding plumage would occur in BIOT. The easiest diagnostic markings to see are any vestiges of black on the underwings in this species. Black Tern has a more extensive "blacker" head in all plumages; Whiskered Tern is a whiter bird with a distinctive shaped head pattern that includes a dark-spotted crown.

LOCAL NOTES: These are birds of the freshwater sewage works on Diego Garcia that are fairly reliably seen in the northern winter months. Look for their smaller size when perched among other terns on the wires that straddle the settling ponds.

Chris Patrick

Brown Noddy *Anous stolidus* (Linnaeus, 1758)

STATUS AND DISTRIBUTION: A common resident: it still breeds individually in trees on most islands of the Territory. However, the large colonies that once occurred have not been recorded in the Territory since 1996. The decline in breeding numbers for Brown Noddy has not been attributable to any cause and is of great concern. In 1975 during a survey of the Great Chagos Bank islands, it was noted as the most numerous species on all the islands except Resurgent and Eagle, neither of which suit Brown Noddy as breeding islands due to the rocky exposed nature of the former and rats being present on the latter. During this survey, Nelsons Island held 16,600 pairs, Danger Island 12,500 pairs, Sea Cow 11,500 pairs, South Brother 7,400 pairs and smaller numbers on Middle and North Brother. In 1996, these islands still held colonies numbering low thousands, though overall breeding numbers had declined. By 2006, the numbers had catastrophically declined. Throughout quarterly surveys between October 2008 and October 2010, that visited all of the known breeding islands, no breeding colonies of this species were located. The reason for this apparent decline is unknown. In fact, so little is known of its breeding strategy in BIOT that it could simply be that protracted periods of non-breeding are normal. It is still a common species throughout the Territory, possibly due to longevity, nowhere more so than Diego Garcia, where it very evident in the coconut trees of Downtown.

IDENTIFICATION GUIDE: Being brown all year and having a wedge-shaped tail means Brown Noddy is a straightforward species to identify to genus, though some care is needed to separate it from Lesser Noddy that also occurs in BIOT. Brown Noddy is a warm chocolate-brown with a duller greyer head patch. It is also larger, looking noticeably bulkier in flight, particularly the chest and with longer wings and bigger bill.

SIMILAR SPECIES: Lesser Noddy is the only other all-brown tern that occurs in BIOT. Once the size of the two species is known, it is possibly the best identification feature, even at range. Lesser Noddy looks daintier and more agile in flight. The striking white fore-crown of Lesser Noddy is a good recognition feature but good views of the bird are required due to the generally intense sun of BIOT distorting the true brightness of the white.

LOCAL NOTES: Mixed feeding flocks of this species offshore along with Red-footed Booby and Lesser Noddy are a great natural spectacle, often seen on boating trips off Diego Garcia. Huge shoals of small fish are driven to the surface by underwater predators where several hundred birds flock to feast on them: the waters are explosive with jumping fish and diving birds.

Pete Carr

Lesser Noddy *Anous tenuirostris* (Temminck, 1823)

Pete Carr

STATUS AND DISTRIBUTION: Nowhere near as numerous as Brown Noddy, except on the islands where it breeds and when feeding flocks are encountered at sea. Similar to the preceding species, Lesser Noddy has declined as a breeding species, noted since the breeding seabirds were first accurately recorded in the 1970s. In March 1996, 43,275 breeding pairs were found: this figure had dropped to 2,682 pairs in March 2006. The situation is complicated because their breeding strategy is not known. In February 2009, there were an estimated 12,750 pairs breeding throughout BIOT; later that year, in July, a further 12,650 pairs were breeding. Whilst this still represents a substantial decline from 1996, it is not as catastrophic as the 2006 counts initially indicated. Long-term standardised monitoring of both noddy species is required to investigate their true criticality and conservation requirements.

IDENTIFICATION GUIDE: A slim and agile bird in flight, its smaller, darker appearance is usually sufficient to identify it. See further notes under Similar Species for both Brown and Lesser Noddy.

SIMILAR SPECIES: In addition to the physical features covered under Brown Noddy, habitat and location can assist with identification. Lesser Noddy is far more uncommon throughout the Territory than Brown Noddy. It is an arboreal colonial breeder: Brown Noddy nest singly in trees and colonially on the ground.

LOCAL NOTES: To see, hear and smell this species breeding in its thousands on bushes and trees is an unforgettable experience. The huge colonies in *Pisonia grandis* trees on Petite Ile Bois Mangue are reminiscent of a Hollywood film-set. The ancient trees are huge, twisted and gnarled and their interwoven canopies block out most light and little grows below them. Several thousand Lesser Noddy breed in these interconnected trees, the noise of chattering birds and smell of guano is extraordinary, as is the way, the exceedingly tame birds come down to investigate any intruder, often hovering within feet of the face of a person.

Pete Carr

Common White Tern *Gygis alba* (Sparrman, 1786)

STATUS AND DISTRIBUTION: A common breeding resident throughout all atolls of the Territory. This beautiful and inquisitive bird is found everywhere, including islands that have been ecologically destroyed by coconut plantations and introduced rats. It is exceedingly difficult to gain an accurate population figure due to it not breeding communally and not building nests, however, the total BIOT breeding population was estimated at 610 pairs in 1996 and 603 in 2006. This estimate had not changed in 2010.

Chris Patrick

IDENTIFICATION GUIDE: Unmistakeable. Its brilliant all-white colouration and very dark, large-looking eyes make it easy to identify, even at long ranges.

LOCAL NOTES: Birds roost communally in the Downtown area of Diego Garcia, seeming to favour Ironwood *Casuarina equisetifolia* trees in well lit areas. Up to 40 birds will gather noisily in a single tree and can frequently be heard calling well after the sun has gone down.

Other seabirds

Bulwer's Petrel *Bulweria bulwerii* (Jardine & Selby, 1828)
A single bird was caught aboard RFA Resurgent off Eagle Island on 18 January 1975. The only other records are of single birds recorded at sea on 17 February 2001, 280 km north of the Chagos Bank at approximately 4°S, 71°E, and again on 18 and 19 February 2001 at 07.0°S, 78.2°E by the vessel CS Romance.

Jouanin's Petrel *Bulweria fallax* Jouanin, 1955
The only record of this species within BIOT waters is of a single bird at sea at 5°23'S, 66°52'E on 26 January 1960.

White-faced Storm-petrel *Pelagodroma marina* (Latham, 1790)
The only confirmed sighting of this species is of a single bird at 06°57'S, 71°44'E on 10 October 1974.

Black-bellied Storm-petrel *Fregetta tropica* (Gould, 1844)
There is a single confirmed sighting of this species in BIOT waters at 5°43'S, 67°26'E on 22 June 1964.

Swinhoe's Storm-petrel *Oceanodroma monorhis* (Swinhoe, 1867)
There is a single record in BIOT waters at 4°45'S, 71°33'E on 18 February 2001.

Red-billed Tropicbird *Phaethon aethereus* Linnaeus, 1758
The only record of this species in the Chagos Archipelago comes from the vessel CS Romance at 4°45'S, 71°33'E on 18 February 2001.

Kelp Gull *Larus dominicanus* Lichtenstein, 1823
A single record exists of a lone bird on Nelsons Island on 07 February 1975. Although the published description is brief, it is adequate to conclusively identify this distinctive species.

Gull-billed Tern *Sterna nilotica* Gmelin, 1789
A single record exists for this species in the Chagos Archipelago; a lone adult bird in non-breeding plumage was seen and photographed on Diego Garcia over several days in May 2005.

Chris Patrick

Chris Patrick

Lesser Crested Tern *Sterna bengalensis* Lesson, 1831
Lesser Crested Tern is an extremely rare species in BIOT. The first records come from Diego Garcia in April and May 1971, followed by two more birds on Diego Garcia, which were photographed on 31 May and 01 June 2005. The latest record is of three birds in Peros Banhos on 05 April 2010.

White-cheeked Tern *Sterna repressa* Hartert, 1916
All records of this species have come from the sewage lagoons on Diego Garcia. The first record is of three birds on 28 May 2005. It appears to be a regular northern winter visitor in very small numbers, the highest count to date is of 11 birds on 23 November 2008. A single bird that did not gain summer plumage was still on Diego Garcia on 27 June 2011.

Pete Carr

Arctic Tern *Sterna paradisaea* Pontoppidan, 1763
All records of Arctic Tern have come from Diego Garcia. The first record was of four birds on 27 March 1996, followed by singles on 05 and 09 August 1997, four birds on 11 and nine 14 August 1997. It was sighted 15 times in May 2005. The next record is of four birds on 08 November 2007. Further records follow of up to three birds in January and November 2009, November 2010 and March 2011. All birds have been in winter plumage and one bird in 1997 was in juvenile plumage. The status of this species remains uncertain in BIOT and the Indian Ocean.

Pomarine Jaeger *Stercorarius pomarinus* (Temminck, 1815)
A single record exists of a bird off the Salomon Islands on 07 October 1974.

Parasitic Jaeger *Stercorarius parasiticus* (Linnaeus, 1758)
A single record exists of two birds passing Diego Garcia on 07 November 2007; photographs were taken of the birds but were of insufficient quality to prove the identification or publish. A full description of the birds has been published and is sufficient to verify the record.

LANDBIRDS

Janet Prushansky

Garganey *Anas querquedula* Linnaeus, 1758

STATUS AND DISTRIBUTION: An annual northern hemisphere winter visitor, mainly to Diego Garcia, in very low numbers. This species was first recorded in BIOT by a Joint Services Expedition, who recorded three birds present on the Egmont Islands on 24 December 1972. In November 2007, four and in November 2008, a maximum of eight birds were on Diego Garcia; the 2008 birds remaining until March 2009. Three birds reappeared on 13 October 2009, the last of these birds, a female, left the island on 08 April 2010. The latest record is of a single bird that dropped in to the Downtown sewage farm on Diego Garcia on 03 October 2010.

Janet Prushansky

IDENTIFICATION GUIDE: Males are very distinctive in breeding plumage, which they moult into in late February and early March. The vast majority of birds seen in BIOT are in non-breeding plumage. The most distinctive feature in non-breeding plumage is the head pattern; males and juveniles have contrasting dark and light areas and the females particularly, have white stripes above and below a black line through the eye.

SIMILAR SPECIES: There have only been two other duck species seen in BIOT, both being extreme rarities. One of these, Northern Pintail, is a possible species for confusion. However, it is larger, looks attenuated and should therefore pose no identification problems.

LOCAL NOTES: It is likely that the majority of records of unidentified ducks from BIOT are of this species. Look for Garganey in the freshwater wetlands at the southern end of the runway on Diego Garcia or any long-lasting flooded area. They are site faithful, remaining on the same pool for months if undisturbed.

Janet Prushansky

Yellow Bittern *Ixobrychus sinensis* (Gmelin, 1789)

STATUS AND DISTRIBUTION: A very rare but seemingly annual northern hemisphere winter visitor. It has only been recorded from the freshwater wetlands on Diego Garcia. It was first recorded in March 2004 when 2–6 individuals were present. The next sighting was of a single bird on 31 October 2008. Intermittent sightings were made of one bird for months after, with three birds being recorded on 29 March and the last sighting of the northern winter on 24 April 2009. The next sighting was of a single bird on 13 October 2009. This individual was joined by a second bird, one of which ended up as road-kill on 03 March 2010. The last sighting of the northern hemisphere winter was on 11 March 2010. This bird is secretive and the wintering population is likely to be marginally higher than recorded.

IDENTIFICATION GUIDE: A distinctive species in any plumage. The bold yellow stripes of juveniles being striking and the general colour of adults distinctive.

LOCAL NOTES: Look for this secretive species in the drainage ditch alongside the main road running south past the runways. They are faithful to feeding areas but are easily disturbed and fly when approached.

Janet Prushansky

Striated Heron *Butorides striata* (Linnaeus, 1758)

STATUS AND DISTRIBUTION: A common breeding resident throughout BIOT, this natural colonist has been noted as being present since records of birds first appeared in the late 1800s. The population on Diego Garcia in August 1997 was estimated at 65 pairs; the Eagle Island population was estimated as low tens in 2005. In 2010, the entire BIOT breeding population is estimated at 300–500 pairs. The distinctive dark juveniles are prominent on Diego Garcia during November and December, indicating a main breeding season commencing in September and finishing by January.

Janet Prushansky

IDENTIFICATION GUIDE: A distinctive species that should not be confused with any other water-bird occurring in BIOT. The yellow legs when standing contrast sharply with the dark body. In flight, the lack of contrast in the upper-wings prevents confusion with Yellow Bittern.

LOCAL NOTES: This is a very vocal species, particularly when alarmed. On Diego Garcia, it is equally at home feeding along the rocky ocean shores or the saltwater barachois as it is on the freshwater ponds and drainage ditches.

Janet Prushansky

Indian Pond-heron *Ardeola grayii* (Sykes, 1832)

STATUS AND DISTRIBUTION: The exact status of this species is still uncertain, it is believed to be an annual visitor in extremely small numbers during the northern hemisphere winter, with occasional birds remaining throughout the year. It was first recorded in BIOT on Diego Garcia on 31 October 2007, when a juvenile was found; a second, adult, bird was seen on Diego Garcia on 04 November 2007. The juvenile was seen again on three further dates in November 2007. The next record is of three birds on Diego Garcia on 23 October 2008 that were seen intermittently up until 24 April 2009. The next sighting on Diego Garcia is of a single bird on 26 October 2009, followed by infrequent sightings of

Janet Prushansky

up to five birds throughout the northern hemisphere winter. One of these birds remained on the island throughout the northern summer months of 2010. Of great interest have been occasional sightings on the northern atolls. There have been records of individual birds on Ile du Coin, Peros Banhos in November 2008 and February 2010 and from Ile Boddam, Salomon Islands in January and July 2009 and February 2010.

IDENTIFICATION GUIDE: This species superficially resembles the much more common Cattle Egret. The distinctive dark back and mantle is easily seen when the birds fly. To date no other pond-herons have been recorded in BIOT, therefore separation from all other herons and egrets should be straightforward.

LOCAL NOTES: This species is spectacular in breeding plumage, only recorded to date in BIOT in November. The purple, dark red-black back contrasting with pure white wings and the amazing multi-coloured bill make it a great find.

Janet Prushansky

White-breasted Waterhen *Amaurornis phoenicurus* (Pennant, 1769)

STATUS AND DISTRIBUTION: A natural colonist and common resident breeder that has to date only been recorded with any certainty on Diego Garcia. This history of the first occurrence of this and the next species is something of a mystery. There are unconfirmed reports of "moorhens" as far back as 1960 from Diego Garcia and Peros Banhos, however it was not until 1995 that it was confirmed that this species was located here. The population on Diego Garcia was estimated in 2010 as a minimum of 100 birds and they are found throughout the island, including the heavily wooded eastern side of the island: the breeding stronghold being the wetlands at the southern end of the runway on the western

Janet Prushansky

side. It breeds throughout the year, with records of chicks in all months, the peak breeding period appearing to be between October and January.

IDENTIFICATION GUIDE: An easy species to observe, particularly along roadsides, the white bellies of the adults being diagnostic and unlike any other bird in BIOT. Chicks of this species can resemble chicks of Common Moorhen, but as they are invariably accompanied by adult birds, their identification through association generally poses no problem.

LOCAL NOTES: White-breasted Waterhen is easiest seen whilst driving the main road from the Air Terminal to the southern end of the runway. Look for them in the drainage ditch running parallel to the road and be wary as they have a fatal habit of running under vehicle wheels with frightening regularity.

Janet Prushansky

Common Moorhen *Gallinula chloropus* (Linnaeus, 1758)

STATUS AND DISTRIBUTION: A natural colonist and a fairly common breeding resident found only on Diego Garcia. The first confirmed record of this species is of 5–6 birds on Diego Garcia in November 2007. Not as widespread or numerous as White-breasted Waterhen, in 2010 the population was estimated to be 10–30 breeding pairs centred upon the flooded borrow pit at San Juan and the brackish wetland at the back of the POL Point. Other pairs can be viewed in the drainage ditches and wetlands around the airfield. The peak breeding season is believed to be between October and January.

IDENTIFICATION GUIDE: A regularly observed and easily identified bird. Much more strictly associated with wetland habitat than the preceding species, the red shield and lack of white breast differentiate it from White-breasted Waterhen. When walking and feeding undisturbed this species has a distinctive bobbing and head-jerking gait.

LOCAL NOTES: Up to 20 birds can regularly be seen feeding on the exposed mud at low tide in the brackish mudflat area between the main road and the POL Point.

Janet Prushansky

Pacific Golden Plover *Pluvialis fulva* (Gmelin, 1789)

STATUS AND DISTRIBUTION: A rare but annual non-breeding northern hemisphere winter visitor, with a very few birds occasionally remaining throughout the year. Almost certainly first recorded in BIOT on 20 November 1972 in the Egmont Islands, when two birds were seen. These birds were recorded as Lesser Golden Plover, as the species had not been separated at that point in time: it is highly likely that these birds were the species now known as Pacific Golden Plover. In the ensuing years, the majority of records have occurred between October and April and are from Diego Garcia. The highest day count has been nine on Diego Garcia on 02 January 2009.

IDENTIFICATION GUIDE: A fairly large, short-billed wader whose overall golden hue, spangled wings and back and well-marked creamy-white supercillium, at any distance should distinguish it.

SIMILAR SPECIES: Grey Plover superficially resembles this species, particularly in shape. In winter plumage, Grey Plover is drab grey and has diagnostic black axillaries when seen in flight.

LOCAL NOTES: Both Grey Plover and Pacific Golden Plover have strong habitat preferences. The former prefers open, saltwater areas and is commonest in the southern barachois of Diego Garcia and on rocky shores throughout BIOT. The latter prefers open grass areas and damp freshwater habitat and is commonest on the golf course and at the edges of flooded grasslands on Diego Garcia.

David Osborn/rspb-images*

Grey Plover *Pluvialis squatarola* (Linnaeus, 1758)

STATUS AND DISTRIBUTION: A fairly common non-breeding northern hemisphere winter visitor with some birds remaining throughout the year; these birds do not assume breeding plumage. It has been recorded throughout the atolls of BIOT, where the highest daily counts have been 26 on 04 November 2007 and 25 on 14 November 2009, both from Diego Garcia.

IDENTIFICATION GUIDE: A large stocky, short-billed shorebird that is noticeably pale grey at any distance. The black axillary (arm-pits) feathers are diagnostic and easily viewed in flight; the plaintive, far carrying "chee-oo-wee" call is also diagnostic and often given in flight.

Janet Pushiansky

SIMILAR SPECIES: See Pacific Golden Plover.

LOCAL NOTES: A bird of oceanic rocky shorelines and saltwater barachois: it is one of the few shorebirds that should be expected to be seen in the outer atolls, especially during the northern hemisphere winter.

Ian Lewis*

Kentish Plover *Charadrius alexandrinus* Linnaeus, 1758

STATUS AND DISTRIBUTION: A rare non-breeding northern hemisphere winter visitor, mainly to Diego Garcia. This species was first recorded in BIOT on the Egmont Islands on 01 January 1973. The only other record away from Diego Garcia is of two birds on Nelsons Island on 14 November 2008. On Diego Garcia, it appears annually in very small numbers: the highest day total being 10 in March 1995. The first birds arrive in October and the latest departing record to date is a single bird on 22 March 2009.

IDENTIFICATION GUIDE: A small, normally pale brown, long dark-legged, short-billed plover with a distinctive white supercillium, white collar and lateral breast patches. In flight it has a clear white wing bar and white sides to the tail.

SIMILAR SPECIES: Two other similar looking plovers have occurred in BIOT: Little Ringed and Common Ringed Plover. Little Ringed has a single breast band, pinkish legs and a yellow eye-ring; Common Ringed is larger, has a breast band and orange-yellow legs.

LOCAL NOTES: It is thought that two subspecies occur in BIOT, the nominate that ranges from Western Europe to Korea and the darker race *seebohmi* that is found in Sri Lanka and southeast India.

Janet Prushansky

Greater Sand Plover *Charadrius leschenaultii* Lesson, 1826

STATUS AND DISTRIBUTION: A common non-breeding northern hemisphere winter visitor to BIOT, with many birds remaining throughout the year. These non-breeding birds do not moult into breeding plumage. Although not noted prior to 1971, it is now a common shorebird throughout BIOT, particularly on the southern barachois of Diego Garcia. The highest day count to date is 65 birds on 25 July 2010 on Diego Garcia; larger numbers are highly likely to be recorded from this island during the northern hemisphere winter.

IDENTIFICATION GUIDE: A large pale brown shorebird with a white belly that is both beautiful and distinctive in summer plumage. However, very few summer plumaged birds are recorded and most are drabber brown and white birds. The size of the bird, its brown colouration and large dark coloured bill should identify it as one of the two Sand Plovers that occur in BIOT – see Similar Species.

SIMILAR SPECIES: A very difficult species to identify to species level due to its similarity to the much rarer Lesser Sand Plover. Greater Sand Plover is usually a larger bird, longer and thicker billed, longer legged, which are normally pale yellow-green and not greyish as in Lesser. The general shape of the head is important, Greater having an angular, sloping forehead, whilst Lesser is a more domed shaped head. When poor views are had, it is safest to leave birds as sand plovers rather than attempt to be specific.

LOCAL NOTES: This is a saltwater habitat bird, which is particularly fond of the barachois on Diego Garcia. They do not congregate in dense flocks and to gain an accurate count of the numbers present would involve a search around the entire area – not an easy task.

Pete Carr

Bar-tailed Godwit *Limosa lapponica* (Linnaeus, 1758)

STATUS AND DISTRIBUTION: An uncommon but regular non-breeding northern hemisphere winter visitor, with some birds remaining throughout the year. Birds remaining all year do not moult into breeding plumage. The first record of this species comes from two birds on Diego Garcia on 01 May 1971. Since then it has been recorded throughout BIOT in all months, the highest daily count to date being 15 birds on Diego Garcia on 31 October 2007.

Janet Prushansky

IDENTIFICATION GUIDE: A large, pale looking, straight-billed shorebird that inhabits the sand-banks of the barachois and wet grasslands. As a godwit, it is unlikely to be confused with anything else apart from the much rarer Black-tailed Godwit – see Similar Species.

SIMILAR SPECIES: Recognition in flight is simplified by the black and white tail and wing pattern of Black-tailed Godwit. When viewed standing, Bar-tailed is smaller, lighter coloured overall and has a less distinctly marked bill: Black-tailed being very obviously fleshy pink at the base and darker towards the tip. Habitat preference is a good indicator of species: on Diego Garcia Black-tailed Godwit avoids saltwater areas and generally stays faithful to a single freshwater patch.

LOCAL NOTES: Turtle Cove and Horseburgh Point lagoons are favourite haunts during dry periods, after prolonged rains they move on to land and feed in open flooded grass areas. They are seldom found on long-lived ponds that are the normal foraging areas of Black-tailed Godwit.

Janet Prushansky

Whimbrel *Numenius phaeopus* (Linnaeus, 1758)

STATUS AND DISTRIBUTION: A common non-breeding northern hemisphere winter visitor to all of BIOT, with some birds remaining throughout the year. This is the most abundant large shorebird and is ubiquitous, seemingly equally at home on golf course, rocky coast, flooded grassland or forest track. The population on Diego Garcia in November 2007 was assessed as in the region of 100 birds, it is likely that the entire BIOT population in the northern hemisphere winter is 300–500.

IDENTIFICATION GUIDE: A fairly straightforward species to identify in BIOT: it is the only large brown wader with a down-curved bill and prominent head-stripes that is likely to be encountered. It has a very distinctive flight contact call of a repeated "di-di-di-di-di-di-di"; it also is the species that will flush first when approached and raises an alarm call similar to the contact call but emitted much louder and more emphatically.

SIMILAR SPECIES: Eurasian Curlew is noted annually in very small numbers and Far Eastern Curlew has been recorded once. Both are noticeably larger and diagnostically their bills are substantially larger: a feature seen from great distance.

LOCAL NOTES: Unusual for a shorebird, this species forages all over the islands in all sorts of habitats. It regularly perches on the branches of dead trees or fence posts; an unusual but regular spectacle on Diego Garcia is up to 20 birds perched on the exposed branches of a single dead tree overlooking Turtle Cove.

Janet Prushansky

Common Greenshank *Tringa nebularia* (Gunnerus, 1767)

STATUS AND DISTRIBUTION: A fairly common northern hemisphere winter visitor throughout BIOT, with some birds remaining throughout the summer months, which do not attain breeding plumage. The highest daily count is of 25 birds on Diego Garcia in November 2009; it is likely that there are up to 100 birds spending the northern hemisphere winter in BIOT.

IDENTIFICATION GUIDE: A large, pale grey wader (in winter plumage) with greenish legs and a long, slightly up-curved bill. It is usually solitary or very occasionally in groups of up to three. Its pale features and distinctive *Tringa* jizz allow this species to be identified at long range.

SIMILAR SPECIES: The very rare Marsh Sandpiper is reminiscent of this species, though is smaller and diagnostically it has a thinner, straighter bill and is normally found in or very near water.

LOCAL NOTES: Ubiquitous in its habitat selection, along with Whimbrel and Ruddy Turnstone, this species should be expected throughout all of BIOT, including the northern islands where yacht crews can land.

Janet Pruslianski

Wood Sandpiper *Tringa glareola* Linnaeus, 1758

STATUS AND DISTRIBUTION: A regular northern hemisphere winter visitor in very small numbers that occurs throughout BIOT where there is freshwater. It arrives in early October and all birds depart north by the end of April. The highest daily count to date is of 15 birds on Diego Garcia on 07 April 2009; the entire BIOT population in the northern hemisphere winter is likely not to exceed 30 birds.

Pete Carr

IDENTIFICATION GUIDE: With good views this species should not be confused with any other bird that occurs in BIOT. It is a strictly freshwater species, never being found in the barachois. It has a distinctive spangled golden-brown plumage with noticeable mustard-yellow legs and a striking supercillium that extends behind the eye. In flight the white rump and slightly barred tail are diagnostic, as is the repeated "chip" alarm call given when flushed.

SIMILAR SPECIES: Green Sandpiper has been recorded twice in BIOT and has a much more dark and white contrast; Common Sandpiper is a regular migrant to BIOT and could therefore be confused with it, though its constant tail-bobbing and bow-winged flight should easily differentiate the two.

LOCAL NOTES: This is a freshwater loving species that is most likely encountered on the drainage ditches of the airfield or on ephemeral rain water ponds. It has never been recorded as spending the northern hemisphere summer months in BIOT.

Alphonse Island Conservation Centre*

Terek Sandpiper *Xenus cinereus* (Güldenstädt, 1775)

STATUS AND DISTRIBUTION: A regular northern hemisphere winter visitor in very small numbers that has, to date, only been recorded on Diego Garcia. Occasional birds have over-summered but these birds do not attain breeding plumage. First recorded in 1971, the highest daily count has been five birds recorded on 01 November 2007.

IDENTIFICATION GUIDE: A distinctive wader, whose flat-backed, elongated, horizontal posture, yellow-red legs and upturned bill make it simple to identify, even at a distance. It is an active feeder and is often noticed in feeding flocks by its constant scurrying around.

SIMILAR SPECIES: Non-breeding plumaged Common Redshank, a very rare visitor to BIOT, has the same general colouration as Terek Sandpiper. Common Redshank has a more upright stance, redder legs and a straight bill.

LOCAL NOTES: Ubiquitous in its selected habitat, this species has been recorded on the lagoon shore, sewage farms and the southern barachois. Its favoured area appears to be Horseburgh Point barachois.

Janet Prushansky

Common Sandpiper *Actitis hypoleucos* Linnaeus, 1758

STATUS AND DISTRIBUTION: A regular northern hemisphere winter visitor in small numbers that is found throughout all of BIOT. It arrives earlier than other migrant waders, with the first birds appearing on Diego Garcia in mid-August. All of these birds have returned north by the end of April. To date, there has been no record of a bird over-summering. The highest daily count is of 10 birds on Diego Garcia on 23 November 2008; the entire wintering BIOT population is likely to be less than 30 birds.

IDENTIFICATION GUIDE: This species has a very characteristic tail-bobbing action that is constant when moving; this makes identification simple at any range. It also has a very distinctive bow-winged, whirring flight and a thin but carrying "see-see-see" call that allows identification at range.

LOCAL NOTES: It utilises two different habitats in BIOT. It can often be found picking insects up from the shoreline of the freshwater sewage settling ponds. It also appears at home in the brackish swamps surrounding Horseburgh Point lagoons, a habitat not dissimilar to mangrove swamps on mainland Asia where this species is regularly found in winter.

Pene Carr

Ruddy Turnstone *Arenaria interpres* (Linnaeus, 1758)

STATUS AND DISTRIBUTION: A common northern hemisphere winter visitor to all of the atolls of BIOT; it is the most widespread of the wintering waders. Many birds remain over the northern hemisphere summer months, with some achieving summer plumage. The highest daily count has been 250 birds on Diego Garcia on 08 April 2010; it is likely that in excess of 1,000 birds are present throughout BIOT during the northern winter.

IDENTIFICATION GUIDE: A distinctive bird in any plumage. The tortoiseshell-like pattern on the back, orange legs and bold black and white wing pattern make this species very obvious and unlike any other that occurs in BIOT.

Janet Prushansky

LOCAL NOTES: Ruddy Turnstone is found in all habitats and appears equally at home in flooded grasslands and rocky shores. It is the most widespread wader in BIOT and can be found on any island, no matter how small.

Janet Prushansky

Sanderling *Calidris alba* (Pallas, 1764)

STATUS AND DISTRIBUTION: A regular northern hemisphere visitor in low numbers to all of the atolls of BIOT. A few individuals remain throughout the northern summer but do not achieve summer plumage; some returning adults do still have vestiges of breeding plumage. The highest daily count is of 23 birds on the Egmont Islands on 27 November 1972.

IDENTIFICATION GUIDE: One of the easier waders to identify that regularly occurs in BIOT. The pale grey plumage of non-breeding birds coupled with the black carpal patch make this active feeder easy to pick out and unlike any other small wader that occurs.

LOCAL NOTES: Sanderling are usually found feeding on sandy shorelines, this is not normally the case in BIOT, most likely due to a lack of suitable beaches. On Diego Garcia, its regular haunts are the sewage farms and sandy areas of the barachois. On the northern atolls, it is regularly found on rocky shores.

Pete Carr

Curlew Sandpiper *Calidris ferruginea* (Pontoppidan, 1763)

STATUS AND DISTRIBUTION: The most numerous of the waders that spend the northern hemisphere winter in BIOT. It can be found throughout all of the atolls, though generally avoids islands with only rocky coastlines. The highest daily count has been 500 birds on Diego Garcia on two dates in October 2009. It is likely that the BIOT population during the northern hemisphere winter is in excess of 1,500 birds.

IDENTIFICATION GUIDE: A fairly nondescript bird out of breeding plumage, fortunately it has a diagnostic down-curved bill that distinguishes it from all other waders that occur in BIOT. The white rump in flight is also an important identification feature.

Janet Prushansky

Non-breeding plumage

LOCAL NOTES: Curlew Sandpipers form the biggest flocks of all the shorebirds wintering in BIOT. They appear to prefer the muddy areas of the barachois for feeding and groups of 50+ birds are regularly recorded in both Turtle Cove and Horseburgh Point lagoons.

Janet Prushansky

Little Stint *Calidris minuta* (Leisler, 1812)

STATUS AND DISTRIBUTION: A regular though very uncommon visitor that was first recorded in BIOT in 1973 on a Joint Services Expedition to the Egmont Islands: it has only been found on Diego Garcia since then. It has been recorded throughout the year, though is likely to be primarily a northern hemisphere winter visitor. The highest daily count has been of six birds on 20 November 2009 and again on 02 April 2010.

IDENTIFICATION GUIDE: This is one of the most difficult species to identify that regularly occurs in BIOT. A tiny, dark legged shorebird, it is relatively straightforward to identify it as a stint – see Similar Species.

SIMILAR SPECIES: Being a tiny and dark-legged wader narrows the bird down to one of four species; Little Stint, Red-necked Stint, Western Sandpiper *Calidris mauri* and Semipalmated Sandpiper *Calidris pusilla*. The latter two have (difficult to see) partly-webbed toes and are unlikely candidates to occur in BIOT being of Nearctic origin. Red-necked Stint is subtly different with a deeper bill that has a slight bulge at the tip, generally less of a breast band, shorter legs and longer wings. Two of the "yellow-legged" stints have also occurred in BIOT, Long-toed and Temminck's. These are incedibly rare and the paler coloured legs are usually sufficient to differentiate them. Any bird not in breeding plumage that is not well viewed should probably be left as indeterminate.

LOCAL NOTES: Fairly ubiquitous in its choice of habitat, it has been found on the edges of sewage settling ponds, ephemeral freshwater ponds and the saltwater barachois of Turtle Cove and Horseburgh Point lagoons.

Chris Patrick

Oriental Pratincole *Glareola maldivarum* Forster, 1795

STATUS AND DISTRIBUTION: A very uncommon but regular northern hemisphere winter visitor to BIOT. This species was first recorded in BIOT in the Egmont Islands where four birds were present between November and December 1972. It was seen again on the Egmont Islands on 28 February 2009. On Diego Garcia, it is normally first found in late October and all birds have departed by the end of March, the latest record being of a single bird seen on 22 March 2009. The maximum count to date is of four birds during the northern hemisphere winter in 1972 and again in 2009.

Chris Patrick

IDENTIFICATION GUIDE: Pratincoles are a unique, crepuscular, aerial feeding family that, when not hunting, spend protracted periods standing motionless on the ground. Being long winged aerobatic birds, pratincoles as a family are easy to identify. The chestnut patches on the underwings lead to either Oriental Pratincole or Collared Pratincole *Glareola pratincola*, which has been recorded once to date on Diego Garcia. Separating these two species requires good views in order to confirm the diagnostic features – see Similar Species.

SIMILAR SPECIES: Collared Pratincole has a longer tail, an indentation to the centre of the black terminal tail band and a white trailing edge to the underwing.

LOCAL NOTES: The birds that have been recorded on Diego Garcia appear to be site faithful. They generally inhabit grass fields that have flooded areas and will remain in the vicinity of their chosen area for the duration of their stay. When flushed they generally only fly a short distance before settling again to resume their motionless stance.

Pete Carr

House Crow *Corvus splendens* Vieillot, 1817

STATUS AND DISTRIBUTION: The status of House Crow in BIOT is currently undetermined. The first record of this most unwelcome invasive pest is from May 2002 on Diego Garcia. A single bird, likely the 2002 individual, was still present in November 2008 and was joined by a second bird on 09 November 2008. The next sighting was of an individual bird on 12 December 2009: over a year later and active coverage of the island was very good throughout this period. In 2010, in January there were three sightings of a single bird and one of two birds together on the 25th; in February there were a further two sightings of a single bird; and March the same. In April, May and June 2010 there were single sightings of two birds together, all from Barton Point. There have been no further sightings of these birds, though it is likely they are still at Barton Point and the restricted access to this area has prevented any further records.

IDENTIFICATION GUIDE: A simple species to identify in BIOT, it is the only crow that occurs. It has a weak high-pitched *corvid*-like call (the most usual way of locating them) and has a diagnostic grey nape when viewed.

LOCAL NOTES: It is very fortunate that the two birds on Diego Garcia appear to be of the same sex as no breeding has occurred to date. This species receives no protection in BIOT and is considered a pest. However, due to its very elusive nature on this island, all attempts at eradication have failed to date.

Other landbirds

Australian Shelduck *Tadorna tadornoides* Jardine & Selby, 1828
An endemic species to southern-Australia and incredibly seven individuals were
found at one of the sewage farms on Diego Garcia in September 2002, with
some birds remaining until at least November 2002. These birds were well
photographed. The origin of these birds is unknown, it is deemed unlikely they
were truly wild birds that made their way to Diego Garcia unassisted by man.

Nestor Guzman

Mallard *Anas platyrhynchos* Linnaeus, 1758
A single male Mallard was photographed by Kathryn Cottier from the yacht "Mr Curly", on a brackish pond on
Ile Boddam, Salomon Islands in May 2009: the exact date was not recorded. The bird was identified from the
photographs and stands as the only confirmed record from the BIOT.

Northern Pintail *Anas acuta* Linnaeus, 1758
An unpublished but confirmed record exists of a single bird with three Garganey, found on 24 December 1972
by Joint Services Expedition to the Egmont Islands. This record is presumably the source of the picture of this
species that appears in the book *Half of Paradise* by Professor David Bellamy.

Claire Jones

Greater Flamingo *Phoenicopterus roseus* Pallas, 1811
There is a historic unconfirmed report of a colony of flamingos at the southern
end of Diego Garcia. All factors considered, it is unlikely this colony ever
permanently existed in the barachois on Diego Garcia, though recent evidence
suggests overshooting migrants may have previously reached BIOT. Mrs Claire
Jones of the yacht "Brumby" handed over
photographs of a flamingo she caught on camera
on 11 April 2007 on Ile Boddam, Salomon Islands: the quality of the five
photographs (one above) is sufficient to identify the bird to species level.

Nestor Guzman

Glossy Ibis *Plegadis falcinellus* (Linnaeus, 1766)
A single bird was recorded by most ornithologists visiting Diego Garcia between
1995 and 2009: it is likely to be the same long-lived bird.

Pete Carr

Cinnamon Bittern *Ixobrychus cinnamomeus* (Gmelin, 1789)
An adult bird was found and photographed beside the main road outside the
landfill site on Diego Garcia, feeding on insects on 12 November 2009. A second
juvenile bird was found and photographed in an area of flooded waste ground
on Diego Garcia on 12 January 2010.

Black-crowned Night-heron *Nycticorax nycticorax* (Linnaeus, 1758)
The first record of this species is of three birds that were present on Diego Garcia in November 2007: a
juvenile, an immature, and a well photographed adult. All other records are from the same island and are a
single bird between 21–24 October 2008, a further single bird on 13 October 2009, two birds on 08 March
2010 and the final sighting to date of four birds at the Landfill Site on 04 October 2010. It is possible that this
species is regular to Diego Garcia in the northern hemisphere winter arriving in October and departing in
March but due to its mainly nocturnal habits, is going unrecorded.

Grey Heron *Ardea cinerea* Linnaeus, 1758
There is a historic record of a possible sighting on 23 February 1899 and the first confirmed sighting is of a
bird present on Diego Garcia on 30 March 1986, recorded by former British Representative Cdr J. Topp RN and
Mr John Maxwell. Further sightings on Diego Garcia have been of a single adult bird between January and

March 2009, a single bird between December 2009 and March 2010, a single adult bird on 04 October 2010 and a juvenile plumaged bird on 01 December 2010. This species appears to be a genuine vagrant to BIOT, with individual birds that have overshot on their southerly migration then staying for the northern hemisphere winter before departing, presumably back north to breed.

Purple Heron *Ardea purpurea* Linnaeus, 1766
A single record exists of a well-photographed bird that was on Diego Garcia from November 2000 to February 2001.

Great Egret *Casmerodius albus* (Linnaeus, 1758)
A single individual was noted in amongst Little and Cattle Egret on 29 March 1996; the next sighting was over a decade later in November 2007, both on Diego Garcia. This bird was possibly the same individual present on the island in October 2008 and was joined by a second individual in February 2009. Both birds were sighted again on 07 March 2009 and had departed the island by 24 April 2009. An individual bird returned to the island on 04 November 2009 and this long staying bird was last sighted on 19 April 2010. The latest record is of another lone bird on Diego Garcia on 04 October 2010. A genuine vagrant to BIOT, those birds that make it to Diego Garcia during northern autumn migration appear to remain there for the northern hemisphere winter before returning north.

Little Egret *Egretta garzetta* (Linnaeus, 1766)
including **Dimorphic Egret** *Egretta dimorpha* Hartert, 1914
There is a single record of a Dimorphic Egret that was found and photographed on Diego Garcia on 01 February 1995. Incredibly, this individual had been ringed, although unfortunately the ringing details were never ascertained. The next record is of up to six Little Egret amongst Cattle Egret and a Great Egret on Diego Garcia in March 1996. Thereafter there are seven records of Little Egret, all from Diego Garcia and all occurring between October and May in the northern hemisphere winter and all relating to either a single or two birds. There are also 12 records between October 2009 and March 2010, which claim to be of Dimorphic Egret. As the taxonomic status of Dimorphic Egret has not been fully accepted and there are challenges in identifying this potential species in the field, it is best to group all of these records together under Little Egret.

Lesser Kestrel *Falco naumanni* Fleischer, 1818
A single record exists of this highly migratory, social falcon that migrates across the western Indian Ocean. A lone bird was found on Diego Garcia on 05 December 2009, it appeared to stay on the island for a very short period and was never relocated after being initially found and photographed. This bird was first thought to be (the expected) Amur Falcon, though was sub sequentially re-identified from an excellent series of photographs by Janet Prushansky.

Amur Falcon *Falco amurensis* Radde, 1863
The first record of these sociable falcons, which migrate across the western Indian Ocean, is of four birds on Diego Garcia in December 2002. The second occurrence is in November 2008, when a flock of 13 were found on Diego Garcia – the last two of this influx was seen on 10 December 2008. A further single bird was photographed on Diego Garcia on 14 November 2009; this increased to three birds by 20 November and the last of this influx was seen on 13 December 2009. The latest sightings have been of an individual at sea off Peros Banhos in late November 2010, photographed by the BIOT Patrol Vessel, Pacific Marlin, and an individual bird on Diego Garcia on 14 December 2010. It is most probable all records of unidentified small raptors seen throughout BIOT are likely to be this species.

Lanner Falcon *Falco biarmicus* Temminck, 1825
Former British Representative Cdr J. Topp RN gives details of a pair that were seen and photographed at Point Marianne, Diego Garcia in February 2002. These birds are likely to have come from captive stock and probably escaped from a ship.

Peregrine Falcon *Falco peregrinus* Tunstall, 1771
There is a record, with photographs, of a Peregrine Falcon picked up dead on the airfield on Diego Garcia on 21 November 2002: the bird's identity being confirmed by the Smithsonian. There is a second record of a bird hunting over the airfield that was photographed on 24 November 2009.

Osprey *Pandion haliaetus* (Linnaeus, 1758)
A single confirmed sighting to date of a lone bird recorded in Peros Banhos by the then British Representative, Commander Chris Moorey RN on 06 September 2010.

White-bellied Sea-eagle *Haliaeetus leucogaster* (Gmelin, 1788)
A single record exists of a lone, presumed sub-adult bird, observed on a single day during 06–09 February 1975 in the Salomon Island lagoon during a Joint Services Expedition.

Pied Harrier *Circus melanoleucos* (Pennant, 1769)
A single juvenile was observed and photographed whilst hunting above the airfield wetlands on Diego Garcia on 12 November 2009. It remained on the island until at least 30 March 2010.

Pete Carr

Pete Carr

Crab Plover *Dromas ardeola* Paykull, 1805
The appearance of Crab Plover as a migrant to BIOT appears to have dramatically declined over the last century. In September and October 1885, it was reported as "common, but shy." More recently, in 1971 on Diego Garcia, there were four records during April and May, including a single day tally of 20 on 01 May. On 11 December 1972, 13 birds were recorded by the Joint Services Expedition to the Egmont Islands: records seriously declined thereafter. In 1995, there are records again on Diego Garcia of two adults and two juveniles in April and a further two adults in July 1995; this is followed by two further birds at Point Marianne on 27 March 1996. The next record is not until 14 November 2009, despite some intense ornithological activity on Diego Garcia in the interim period. The latest records are of an adult bird found and photographed in Turtle Cove on 28 April 2010, followed by intermittent records of a juvenile bird on the same island throughout 2010.

Common Ringed Plover *Charadrius hiaticula* Linnaeus, 1758
The first record in BIOT is of a lone bird in the Egmont Islands on 08 December 1972 and presumably the same bird on 01 January 1973, recorded by the Joint Services Expedition. The next record is of an individual bird on Diego Garcia on 08 November 2007. This is followed by a record of a bird that was found on Diego Garcia on 20 October 2009 that was joined by a second bird on 13 November 2009. The last report was of presumably one of these two birds on 31 March 2010.

Janet Prushansky

Little Ringed Plover *Charadrius dubius* Scopoli, 1786
Two records exist to date: both from Diego Garcia. The first is a bird photographed and identified by Janet Prushansky on 30 December 2009, followed by a second bird on 28 February 2010. Both birds were located on a freshwater pool in the vicinity of the air terminal.

Pete Carr*

Lesser Sand Plover *Charadrius mongolus* Pallas, 1776

The true status of this species in BIOT is likely to be masked by the difficulties involved in positively identifying it from Greater Sand Plover. The first certain records are from the Joint Services Expedition to the Egmont Island in 1972/73, which recorded a maximum of eight on 04 January 1973. From Diego Garcia there are over 30 records dating back to 1995, all of the birds sighted between October and April in the northern hemisphere winter; the highest daily count being 15 birds on 02 April 2010. It is very likely this species is a regular northern hemisphere visitor to BIOT in limited numbers.

Pintail Snipe *Gallinago stenura* (Bonaparte, 1830)

Pete Carr

Unidentified snipe species have been seen in BIOT as far back as 1905, when the Percy Sladen Trust Expedition noted one in July. There is a record of two birds in March 1995 that was identified most probably as Pintail Snipe. On 18 January 2009, two snipe were noted feeding over an ephemeral pond on Diego Garcia, a net was set over the pond and at dawn the following day one of the birds was caught. In the hand, the diagnostic tail feathers and underwing pattern proved conclusively that these birds were *G. stenura* and were photographed. One of these birds was seen in the same spot over the following two days. There are further records of a single bird on 29 March and 02 April 2009 that possibly relate to the January birds. There were a further two birds on Diego Garcia on 21 November 2009 and the latest sighting was of a single bird at the Landfill Site on 01 December 2010.

Common Snipe *Gallinago gallinago* (Linnaeus, 1758)

Pete Carr

On 05 November 2007, a snipe was photographed on Diego Garcia; the photographs show the diagnostic pale narrow brow in front of the eye and white belly of Common Snipe and proved the first confirmed record for BIOT. Since then, there have been a further 28 records on Diego Garcia, all occurring between October and March in the northern hemisphere winter. The highest daily count has been of five birds on the 22 and 23 November 2009.

Black-tailed Godwit *Limosa limosa* (Linnaeus, 1758)

Pete Carr
Janet Prushansky

The first record of this species is of three non-breeding plumaged birds on Diego Garcia foraging with other shorebirds, including Bar-tailed Godwit, on 25 and 30 July 1995. The next record is of a single bird found on Diego Garcia on 13 October 2009. This bird was joined by a second on 29 October 2009 and the two birds were seen intermittently until 28 March 2010. The remaining individual bird was last seen on the island on 02 June 2010.

Eurasian Curlew *Numenius arquata* (Linnaeus, 1758)

The earliest report of this species is of a bird being shot on Diego Garcia in December 1960. This is followed by two birds sighted on the Egmont Islands in November 1972. All records thereafter are from Diego Garcia, where four birds were together on 06 October 1974: still the highest daily count. The next individual was recorded on 06 March 2004, followed by and one or more likely two birds on 08 November 2007. From October 2009 through to October 2010 (the latest records included), there have been 22 further records covering all months and involving up to two birds. A picture is emerging that this species may be a regular northern hemisphere winter visitor to BIOT in extremely small numbers.

Far Eastern Curlew *Numenius madagascariensis* (Linnaeus, 1766)
A single bird on Diego Garcia was recorded between 04–06 November 2007. This bird was initially thought to be a Eurasian Curlew, however, examination of a series of photographs and field notes revealed the exceedingly long bill and dark barred underwings; the diagnostic features of Far Eastern Curlew. In the field, the call was immediately noticeable as different from Eurasian Curlew.

Spotted Redshank *Tringa erythropus* (Pallas, 1764)
There are three records to date, all from Diego Garcia. The first two birds were recorded on 19 and 21 March 1995. The only subsequent record is of another two birds seen at Horseburgh Point lagoons on 27 May 2005.

Common Redshank *Tringa totanus* (Linnaeus, 1758)
First found in BIOT on 10 November 1972 in the Egmont Islands by the Joint Services Expedition. All subsequent records have come from Diego Garcia. The next record is of a single bird on 19 and 23 March 1995. The only subsequent records are of a single bird on 01 and 06 November 2007 and two birds on 02 November 2007.

Marsh Sandpiper *Tringa stagnatilis* (Bechstein, 1803)
This species was first recorded in BIOT on Ile Boddam in the Salomon Islands on 08 October 1974. Subsequent records are of two birds at Horseburgh Point lagoons on Diego Garcia on 30 May 2005 and another individual there on 01 November 2007. A single bird was present on Diego Garcia between 20 November 2009 and 01 April 2010.

Janet Prushansky

Green Sandpiper *Tringa ochropus* Linnaeus, 1758
A single bird was seen on five occasions on Diego Garcia between 01 February and 03 March 2009.

Chris Patrick

Grey-tailed Tattler *Heteroscelus brevipes* (Vieillot, 1816)
The first confirmed record of this species is of a single bird found on Diego Garcia on 20 March 1995. Subsequent records are of a single bird on Diego Garcia during 26–29 March 1996, another on West Island on 05 and 09 August 1997 and a final photographed bird on Diego Garcia on 03 and 04 November 2007.

Red-necked Stint *Calidris ruficollis* (Pallas, 1776)
There are claims of this species on Diego Garcia in March 1995, August 1996 and May 2005. The former two records have no associated substantiating data and the photographs of the May 2005 bird have subsequently proven it to be Little Stint. There is one accepted record to date: a lone individual appeared on Diego Garcia on 12 November 2009 and was well-photographed. These photographs have been passed to international authorities on stint identification and the bird has been authenticated as Red-necked Stint.

Pete Carr

Temminck's Stint *Calidris temminckii* (Leisler, 1812)
The first record of this species in BIOT is of a bird on board a ship at 06°57'S, 71°44'E on 10 October 1974. The only other record is of an individual bird that stayed faithful to a freshwater wetland on Diego Garcia between 05 January and 13 February 2009.

Janet Prushansky

Long-toed Stint *Calidris subminuta* (Middendorff, 1853)
The first record of this species in BIOT is of an individual found on Diego Garcia on 20 October 2009. This bird or another was joined by two more on 12 November 2009, these three birds dwindled to two on 15 November and then to one by 24 November 2009. The remaining individual was recorded intermittently on the island until 08 April 2010.

Pectoral Sandpiper *Calidris melanotos* (Vieillot, 1819)

The first record of this species is of a single well-photographed bird on Diego Garcia on 31 October 2007; this bird was joined by a second the following day. A single bird was again recorded on 04 and 08 November 2007. The next record is of a single bird found at the Downtown sewage works on Diego Garcia on 20 January 2009, followed by a long-staying individual again on Diego Garcia: first found on 14 October 2009 and last recorded on 06 November 2009.

Sharp-tailed Sandpiper *Calidris acuminata* (Horsfield, 1821)

A single well-photographed bird with a damaged leg was first sighted on Diego Garcia on 20 October 2009. This bird was joined by a second on 30 October 2009 and these two birds were sighted intermittently until 09 November 2009. One of these individuals remained on island until 13 December 2009. The latest record is of an individual bird found on Horseburgh Point lagoons on 02 October 2010.

Dunlin *Calidris alpina* (Linnaeus, 1758)

There are two records of this species, both from the Joint Services Expedition to the Egmont Islands. Single birds were found on 29 November 1972 and on 06 January 1973.

Ruff *Philomachus pugnax* (Linnaeus, 1758)

The first record of Ruff is of a single well-photographed bird at the landfill site on Diego Garcia on 05 November 2007, which was also seen the following day. The next record is of an individual on Diego Garcia on 02 November 2008, and was joined by a second bird on 26 November 2008: one of these birds remaining on island until 21 January 2009. The next BIOT bird arrived on Diego Garcia on 20 October 2009 and appeared to stay until 24 November 2009. The latest record is of a single bird on Diego Garcia on 03 October 2010.

Red-necked Phalarope *Phalaropus lobatus* (Linnaeus, 1758)

The first record in BIOT of this species is of a bird that was trapped and ringed as part of the Joint Services Expedition to the Egmont Islands (the bird being ringed on 12 January 1973). A second very well-photographed winter plumaged "spinning bird" was on Diego Garcia on 13 and 14 November 2009.

Collared Pratincole *Glareola pratincola* (Linnaeus, 1766)

A single Collared Pratincole was present with Oriental Pratincole on Diego Garcia from 26 December 2009 to 08 March 2010. The bird was initially identified as an Oriental Pratincole: this oversight was pointed out by Janet Prushansky and proven by her excellent series of photographs. This is the first record for BIOT.

Small Pratincole *Glareola lactea* Temminck, 1820

A single record exists of a lone bird seen by the Joint Services Expedition to the Egmont Islands in 1972/3, the exact date has not been ascertained as of yet. This bird is presumably the source of the drawing of this species that appears in the book *Half of Paradise* by Professor David Bellamy

Rock Pigeon (Feral Pigeon) *Columba livia* Gmelin, 1789

A single record to date of what surely must have been a ship-assisted occurrence of this bird on Diego Garcia on 17 September 2009. The bird was seen flying in over the lagoon of Diego Garcia and circle the jetty area before disappearing inland. This bird proved to be extremely tame, accepting rice from people. The last record of this bird was on 14 October 2010.

White-throated Needletail *Hirundapus caudacutus* (Latham, 1802)
Two "needletail" swifts were present on Diego Garcia during 03–08 November 2007. Identification in the field was never achieved due to light conditions and the aerobatic antics of these birds. One of these birds, however, was eventually satisfactorily captured on camera, which facilitated its identification and is a testimony to the tenacity of the cameraman, Chris Patrick.

Common Swift *Apus apus* (Linnaeus, 1758)
There are historic records of swifts occurring in BIOT that were never identified to species level, understandable due to their aerobatic feeding nature and drab plumage. A single bird was recorded on Diego Garcia over the period 03–08 November 2007 and was well-photographed. A combination of the photographs and field descriptions allowed this bird to be safely identified as Common Swift. Subsequent intense ornithological observations on Diego Garcia have produced another 10 records of this species, involving up to three birds: all of these birds occurring in October or November. Two birds were sighted over the Egmont Islands' lagoon on 30 October 2009 and presumably it was these same two birds that were found on Diego Garcia further south on 01 November 2010.

Fork-tailed Swift *Apus pacificus* (Latham, 1802)
A single, photographed bird was recorded on Diego Garcia over the period 03–08 November 2007; this was the first record for BIOT. The second record is of five birds found by the then British Representative, Cdr C. Moorey RN, on 07 May 2010, these birds remaining until 14 May 2010.

European Roller *Coracias garrulus* Linnaeus, 1758
A single juvenile was found and well photographed on Diego Garcia on 19 November 2009. This brief visitor remained on island until 22 November 2009.

Eurasian Hoopoe *Upupa epops* Linnaeus, 1758
A single record exists of a bird in the Downtown area of Diego Garcia in March 1996 – the exact date of occurrence is not recorded.

Barn Swallow *Hirundo rustica* Linnaeus, 1758
There are tentative sightings of this species on Diego Garcia back as far as 1905, when the Percy Sladen Trust Expedition visited the area. All confirmed records to date are from Diego Garcia: the first sighting being a single bird on 09 November 2008; further records are of a lone bird between 18–21 January 2009. The next record is of two birds on 02 November 2009, one of which was still present on 06 November 2009. The final record is of a juvenile plumaged bird on 17 February 2010 hawking over the settling ponds of the Downtown sewage works.

Rosy Starling *Sturnus roseus* (Linnaeus, 1758)
Three Rosy Starlings were present on Diego Garcia from 17 November 2009 to 28 December 2009. They associated with Common Myna and were adults in a transitional plumage. Photographs of a poor quality were taken.

Yellow Wagtail *Motacilla flava* Linnaeus, 1758
The first record is of a single bird found and identified in the Downtown area of Diego Garcia by Lt Cdr Gary Lewis RN, a visiting Royal Navy Birdwatching Society member on 02 June 2005. The next record is a photographed juvenile bird at the Downtown sewage works on 01 November 2007; this individual being joined on the island by a second on 08 November 2009. The latest record is of an individual bird being recorded by the then British Representative, Cdr Chris Moorey RN, on 24 October 2010.

Grey Wagtail *Motacilla cinerea* Tunstall, 1771
There is a single record of an individual bird on Diego Garcia on 30 April and 01 May 2003.

CHAPTER SIX

Checklist of the birds of the British Indian Ocean Territory

"At the present time the information is insufficient to provide a full account of the ornithology of the group, and in the attempt to assess the character of its avifauna there has had to be a strong speculative element." (Dr Bill Bourne summarising the avian knowledge of the Chagos Archipelago in 1971).

Dr Bill Bourne, when summarising in Atoll Research Bulletin, all that was known about the birds of the Chagos Archipelago in 1971, stated that "....there has had to be a strong speculative element [when assessing what was known about certain species]...." Fortunately, in the ensuing four decades, the need for speculation on the present day avifauna has been greatly reduced. BIOT ornithological knowledge is now just entering the stage in which the species that are present, their distribution, their dates of normal occurrence and their breeding phenology is generally known.

In order to produce the present checklist, a search was conducted to locate all Chagos ornithological records post Dr Bourne's seminal 1971 publication. These records have been consolidated to produce the checklist and Table 2. The checklist is of species that, in the author's opinion, have definitely occurred in BIOT. Table 2 gives details of birds that have been reported in BIOT but which, for a variety of reasons, could not unequivocally be included in the present day avifauna. This list includes species that were introduced but have failed to sustain a wild population, e.g. Grey Francolin *Francolinus pondicerianus* (Gmelin, 1789), as well as records that did not permit species level identification, e.g. guineafowl *Numididae* sp. Further to this, it contains records that had inadequate supporting details, often involving species that are either notoriously difficult to identify in the field, were well outside their expected geographic range or were international rarities. Having a record placed in this category does not indicate any doubt about the observer's abilities, rather it demonstrates the requirement for better documentation: a quality photograph or a specimen.

The key factor in producing the two tables was the ability to correctly interpret the records available. In this respect, whilst opinion was sought as to the validity of some of the more challenging records, the ultimate responsibility for which category a record was placed in lies with the author. The guiding principle applied in all cases where any doubt existed about a record's validity has been to err on the side of caution and place a record in Table 2, secure in the knowledge that future research in the area will eventually reveal the true status of a species.

The checklist of the birds of the British Indian Ocean Territory follows overleaf. A brief account for each species in the checklist is contained in Chapter Five and further details of all species that have occurred in BIOT are on **www.worldbirds.org**. Taxonomy and nomenclature follow BirdLife International 2008.

Legend: **?** = Status or date of occurrence uncertain

O = Occurs very exceptionally (<10 birds ever) or involves long-staying individual birds

● = Occurs annually in very low numbers (generally <10 birds/year)

■ = Occurs annually or resident (generally <100 birds)

▮ = Occurs annually or resident (generally >100 birds)

[1] Recorded from Diego Garcia only
[2] Recorded only at sea
[3] Recorded from northern atolls only
[4] Recorded in all appropriate habitat throughout the Territory

Species	Status	J	F	M	A	M	J	J	A	S	O	N	D
Red Junglefowl (domestic chicken) *Gallus gallus* [4]	Introduced resident	■	■	■	■	■	■	■	■	■	■	■	■
Australian Shelduck *Tadorna tadornoides* [1]	Vagrant									○	○	○	
Mallard *Anas platyrhynchos* [3]	Vagrant					○							
Northern Pintail *Anas acuta* [3]	Vagrant	?	?	?									○
Garganey *Anas querquedula* [4]	Non-breeding visitor	●	●	●	●						●	●	●
Wedge-tailed Shearwater *Puffinus pacificus* [4]	Breeding resident	■	■	■	■	■	■	■	■	■	■	■	■
Flesh-footed Shearwater *Puffinus carneipes* [2]	Non-breeding visitor	○	○	○	○	○	?	○	?	?	○	○	
Audubon's Shearwater *Puffinus lherminieri* inc. **Tropical Shearwater** *Puffinus bailloni* [4]	Breeding resident	■	■	■	■	■	■	■	■	■	■	■	■
Bulwer's Petrel *Bulweria bulwerii* [2]	Vagrant	○	○										
Jouanin's Petrel *Bulweria fallax* [2]	Vagrant	○											
Wilson's Storm-petrel *Oceanites oceanicus* [2]	Non-breeding visitor	○	○	○	○	○	○	○	○	○	○	○	○
White-faced Storm-petrel *Pelagodroma marina* [2]	Vagrant										○		
Black-bellied Storm-petrel *Fregetta tropica* [2]	Vagrant						○						
Swinhoe's Storm-petrel *Oceanodroma monorhis* [2]	Vagrant			○									
Greater Flamingo *Phoenicopterus roseus* [3]	Vagrant				○								
Glossy Ibis *Plegadis falcinellus* [1]	Vagrant	○	○	○	○	○	○	○	○	○	○	○	○
Yellow Bittern *Ixobrychus sinensis* [1]	Non-breeding visitor	●	●	●	●						●	●	●
Cinnamon Bittern *Ixobrychus cinnamomeus* [1]	Vagrant	○										○	?
Black-crowned Night-heron *Nycticorax nycticorax* [1]	Vagrant	?	?	○							○	○	?

Species	Status	J	F	M	A	M	J	J	A	S	O	N	D
Striated Heron *Butorides striata* [4]	Breeding resident	■	■	■	■	■	■	■	■	■	■	■	■
Indian Pond-heron *Ardeola grayii* [4]	Non-breeding resident	●	●	●	●	●	●	●	●	●	●	●	●
Cattle Egret *Bubulcus ibis* [4]	Introduced resident	■	■	■	■	■	■	■	■	■	■	■	■
Grey Heron *Ardea cinerea* [1]	Vagrant	○	○	○					○	○	○	?	○
Purple Heron *Ardea purpurea* [1]	Vagrant	○	○									○	○
Great Egret *Casmerodius albus* [1]	Vagrant	○	○	○	○					○	○	○	
Little Egret *Egretta garzetta* [1] inc. **Dimorphic Egret** *Egretta dimorpha* [1]	Vagrant	○	○	○	○					○	○	○	
Red-billed Tropicbird *Phaethon aethereus* [2]	Vagrant										○		
Red-tailed Tropicbird *Phaethon rubricauda* [4]	Breeding resident	■	■	■	■	■	■	■	■	■	■	■	■
White-tailed Tropicbird *Phaethon lepturus* [4]	Breeding resident	■	■	■	■	■	■	■	■	■	■	■	■
Greater Frigatebird *Fregata minor* [4]	Breeding resident	■	■	■	■	■	■	■	■	■	■	■	■
Lesser Frigatebird *Fregata ariel* [4]	Breeding resident	■	■	■	■	■	■	■	■	■	■	■	■
Masked Booby *Sula dactylatra* [3]	Breeding resident	■	■	■	■	■	■	■	■	■	■	■	■
Red-footed Booby *Sula sula* [4]	Breeding resident	■	■	■	■	■	■	■	■	■	■	■	■
Brown Booby *Sula leucogaster* [4]	Breeding resident	■	■	■	■	■	■	■	■	■	■	■	■
Lesser Kestrel *Falco naumanni* [1]	Vagrant											○	
Amur Falcon *Falco amurensis* [1]	Vagrant											●	●
Lanner Falcon *Falco biarmicus* [1]	Vagrant		○										
Peregrine Falcon *Falco peregrinus* [1]	Vagrant											○	

Species	Status	J	F	M	A	M	J	J	A	S	O	N	D
Osprey *Pandion haliaetus* [3]	Vagrant									○			
White-bellied Sea-eagle *Haliaeetus leucogaster* [3]	Vagrant		○										
Pied Harrier *Circus melanoleucos* [1]	Vagrant	○	○	○								○	○
White-breasted Waterhen *Amaurornis phoenicurus* [1]	Breeding resident	■	■	■	■	■	■	■	■	■	■	■	■
Common Moorhen *Gallinula chloropus* [1]	Breeding resident	■	■	■	■	■	■	■	■	■	■	■	■
Crab Plover *Dromas ardeola* [4]	Vagrant	●	●	●	●	●	●	●	●	●	●	●	●
Pacific Golden Plover *Pluvialis fulva* [4]	Non-breeding visitor	●	●	●	●	○	○	○	○	○	●	●	●
Grey Plover *Pluvialis squatarola* [4]	Non-breeding visitor	■	■	■	■	●	●	●	●	●	■	■	■
Common Ringed Plover *Charadrius hiaticula* [4]	Vagrant	○	○	○							○	○	○
Little Ringed Plover *Charadrius dubius* [1]	Vagrant	?	○										○
Kentish Plover *Charadrius alexandrinus* [4]	Non-breeding visitor	●	●	●							○	●	●
Lesser Sand Plover *Charadrius mongolus* [4]	Non-breeding visitor	●	●	●	●	○	○	○	○	○			
Greater Sand Plover *Charadrius leschenaultii* [4]	Non-breeding visitor	■	■	■	■	■	■	■	■	■	■	■	■
Pintail Snipe *Gallinago stenura* [1]	Vagrant	○	○	○	○							○	○
Common Snipe *Gallinago gallinago* [1]	Vagrant	○	○	○							○	○	○
Black-tailed Godwit *Limosa limosa* [1]	Vagrant	○	○	○	○	○	○	○	○	○	○	○	○
Bar-tailed Godwit *Limosa lapponica* [4]	Non-breeding visitor	■	■	■	●	●	●	●	●	●	■	■	■
Whimbrel *Numenius phaeopus* [4]	Non-breeding visitor	■	■	■	■	■	■	■	■	■	■	■	■
Eurasian Curlew *Numenius arquata* [4]	Vagrant	○	○	○	○	○	○	○	○	○	○	○	○
Far Eastern Curlew *Numenius madagascariensis* [1]	Vagrant										○		

Species	Status	J	F	M	A	M	J	J	A	S	O	N	D
Spotted Redshank *Tringa erythropus* [1]	Vagrant			○		○							
Common Redshank *Tringa totanus* [4]	Vagrant			○								○	
Marsh Sandpiper *Tringa stagnatilis* [4]	Vagrant	○	○	○	○	○					○	○	○
Common Greenshank *Tringa nebularia* [4]	Non-breeding visitor	●	●	●	●	●	○	○	○	○	●	●	●
Green Sandpiper *Tringa ochropus* [1]	Vagrant		○	○									
Wood Sandpiper *Tringa glareola* [4]	Non-breeding visitor	●	●	●	●					○	●	●	●
Terek Sandpiper *Xenus cinereus* [1]	Non-breeding visitor	○	○	○	○	○	○	○	○	○	○	○	○
Common Sandpiper *Actitis hypoleucos* [4]	Non-breeding visitor	■	■	■	■				○	○	■	■	■
Grey-tailed Tattler *Heteroscelus brevipes* [1]	Vagrant			○				○			○		
Ruddy Turnstone *Arenaria interpres* [4]	Non-breeding visitor	■	■	■	■	■	■	■	■	■	■	■	■
Sanderling *Calidris alba* [4]	Non-breeding visitor	●	●	●	●	○	○	○	○	○	●	●	●
Little Stint *Calidris minuta* [4]	Non-breeding visitor	○	○	○	○	○	○	○	○	○	○	○	○
Red-necked Stint *Calidris ruficollis* [1]	Vagrant										○		
Temminck's Stint *Calidris temminckii* [1,2]	Vagrant	○	○								○		
Long-toed Stint *Calidris subminuta* [1]	Vagrant	○	○	○	○						○	○	?
Pectoral Sandpiper *Calidris melanotos* [1]	Vagrant	○	○								○	○	?
Sharp-tailed Sandpiper *Calidris acuminata* [1]	Vagrant										○	○	○
Dunlin *Calidris alpina* [3]	Vagrant	○									○		
Curlew Sandpiper *Calidris ferruginea* [4]	Non-breeding visitor	■	■	■	■	■	■	■	■	■	■	■	■
Ruff *Philomachus pugnax* [1]	Vagrant	○	○								○	○	○

Species	Status	J	F	M	A	M	J	J	A	S	O	N	D
Red-necked Phalarope *Phalaropus lobatus* [4]	Vagrant	○										○	
Collared Pratincole *Glareola pratincola* [1]	Vagrant	○	○	○									○
Oriental Pratincole *Glareola maldivarum* [4]	Vagrant	○	○	○							○	○	○
Small Pratincole *Glareola lactea* [3]	Vagrant	?											?
Kelp Gull *Larus dominicanus* [3]	Vagrant		○										
Gull-billed Tern *Sterna nilotica* [1]	Vagrant						○						
Lesser Crested Tern *Sterna bengalensis* [1]	Vagrant				○	○	○						
Great Crested Tern *Sterna bergii* [4]	Breeding resident	■	■	■	■	■	■	■	■	■	■	■	■
Roseate Tern *Sterna dougallii* [4]	Breeding resident	○	○	○	○	○	○	○	○	○	○	○	○
Black-naped Tern *Sterna sumatrana* [4]	Breeding resident	■	■	■	■	■	■	■	■	■	■	■	■
Common Tern *Sterna hirundo* [4]	Vagrant	○	○	○	○	○	?	?	○	○	○	○	○
Arctic Tern *Sterna paradisaea* [4]	Vagrant	○	?	○	?	○	?	?	○	?	?	○	?
Little Tern *Sterna albifrons* [4] inc. **Saunders's Tern** *Sterna saundersi* [1]	Breeding resident / Vagrant	■	■	■	■	■	■	■	■	■	■	■	■
White-cheeked Tern *Sterna repressa* [1]	Vagrant	○	○	○	○	○					○	○	○
Bridled Tern *Sterna anaethetus* [4]	Breeding resident	■	■	■	■	■	■	■	■	■	■	■	■
Sooty Tern *Sterna fuscata* [4]	Breeding resident	■	■	■	■	■	■	■	■	■	■	■	■
White-winged Tern *Chlidonias leucopterus* [1]	Vagrant	○	○	○	○	○					○	○	○
Brown Noddy *Anous stolidus* [4]	Breeding resident	■	■	■	■	■	■	■	■	■	■	■	■
Lesser Noddy *Anous tenuirostris* [4]	Breeding resident	■	■	■	■	■	■	■	■	■	■	■	■

Species	Status	J	F	M	A	M	J	J	A	S	O	N	D
Common White Tern *Gygis alba* [4]	Breeding resident	■	■	■	■	■	■	■	■	■	■	■	■
Pomarine Jaeger *Stercorarius pomarinus* [3]	Vagrant										O		
Parasitic Jaeger *Stercorarius parasiticus* [1]	Vagrant											O	
Rock Pigeon (Feral Pigeon) *Columba livia* [1]	Vagrant										O	O	
Madagascar Turtle-dove *Nesoenas picturata* [1]	Introduced resident	■	■	■	■	■	■	■	■	■	■	■	■
Zebra Dove *Geopelia striata* [1]	Introduced resident	■	■	■	■	■	■	■	■	■	■	■	■
White-throated Needletail *Hirundapus caudacutus* [1]	Vagrant											O	
Common Swift *Apus apus* [4]	Vagrant										O	O	
Fork-tailed Swift *Apus pacificus* [1]	Vagrant				O							O	
European Roller *Coracias garrulus* [1]	Vagrant											O	
Eurasian Hoopoe *Upupa epops* [1]	Vagrant			O									
House Crow *Corvus splendens* [1]	Non-breeding resident	O	O	O	O	O	O	O	O	O	O	O	O
Barn Swallow *Hirundo rustica* [1]	Vagrant	O	O									O	?
Common Myna *Acridotheres tristis* [1]	Introduced resident	■	■	■	■	■	■	■	■	■	■	■	■
Rosy Starling *Sturnus roseus* [1]	Vagrant										O	O	
House Sparrow *Passer domesticus* [3]	Extinct?	?	?	?	?	?	?	?	?	?	?	?	?
Madagascar Red Fody *Foudia madagascariensis* [4]	Introduced resident	■	■	■	■	■	■	■	■	■	■	■	■
Yellow Wagtail *Motacilla flava* [1]	Vagrant						O				O	O	
Grey Wagtail *Motacilla cinerea* [1]	Vagrant				O	O							

Table 2. A checklist of the birds that have historic records but are not accepted as having occurred "beyond reasonable doubt" or, did occur but have died out from the British Indian Ocean Territory. A brief discussion of these records follows the table. Taxonomy and nomenclature follow BirdLife International (2008).

Species	Comment
Guineafowl sp. *Numididae* sp.	A failed introduction
Grey Francolin *Francolinus pondicerianus* (Gmelin, 1789)	A failed introduction
Common Teal *Anas crecca* Linnaeus, 1758	Erroneously named in original paper – should be "Garganey Teal"
Giant Petrel *Macronectes* sp.	Specimen not identifiable to species level
Southern Fulmar *Fulmarus glacialoides* (Smith, 1840)	Insufficient evidence to support record
Broad-billed Prion *Pachyptila vittata* (Forster, 1777)	Insufficient evidence to support record
Gadfly petrels *Pterodroma* sp.	Identification not made to species level
White-bellied Storm-petrel *Fregetta grallaria* (Vieillot, 1817)	Insufficient evidence to support records
Matsudaira's Storm-petrel *Oceanodroma matsudairae* Kuroda, 1922	Insufficient evidence to support records
Western Reef-egret *Egretta gularis* (Bosc, 1792)	Insufficient evidence to support record – record withdrawn
Abbott's Booby *Papasula abbotti* Ridgway, 1893	Insufficient evidence to support records
Pelican sp. *Pelecanidae* sp.	Identification not made to species level
Sparrowhawk sp *Accipitridae* sp.	Identification not made to species level
Great Snipe *Gallinago media* (Latham, 1787)	Author acknowledged identification uncertain
Asian Dowitcher *Limnodromus semipalmatus* (Blyth, 1848)	Insufficient evidence to support record
Spotted Greenshank *Tringa guttifer* (Nordmann, 1835)	Insufficient evidence to support record
Wandering Tattler *Heteroscelus incanus* (Gmelin, 1789)	Insufficient evidence to support record
Lesser Black-backed Gull sp. *Larus fuscus* sp.	Identification not made to species level due to taxonomic problems
Whiskered Tern *Chlidonias hybrida* (Pallas, 1811)	Insufficient evidence to support record
Black Tern *Chlidonias niger* (Linnaeus, 1758)	Insufficient evidence to support record
Great Skua *Catharacta skua* Brünnich, 1764	Insufficient evidence to support record
Pigeon sp. *Columbidae* sp.	Identification not made to species level
Little Swift *Apus affinis* (Gray, 1830)	Insufficient evidence to support record
Pied Crow *Corvus albus* Müller, 1776	Insufficient evidence to support record
Northern House-martin *Delichon urbicum* (Linnaeus, 1758)	Insufficient evidence to support record
Bulbul sp. *Pycnonotidae* sp.	Insufficient evidence to support record
Golden-crested Myna *Ampeliceps coronatus* Blyth, 1842	Record withdrawn

Notes on Table 2

Birds that have historic records of but are not accepted as having occurred "beyond reasonable doubt" or did occur but have died out in BIOT.

Guineafowl sp. *Numididae* sp.

A guineafowl, likely to have been Helmeted Guineafowl *Numida meleagris* (Linnaeus, 1758) was found in the Salomon Islands in 1905 by the Percy Sladen Expedition: it has never been reported since.

Grey Francolin *Francolinus pondicerianus* (Gmelin, 1789)

This species was recorded on Diego Garcia in 1960 and was possibly still there in 1964. The possible 1964 record was the last potential sighting and it has certainly died out in BIOT.

Common Teal *Anas crecca* Linnaeus, 1758

There is a record of three female and a drake "Garganey Teal (*Anas crecca*)" in March 1995. It is certain that these records refer to Garganey *Anas querquedula* Linnaeus, 1758 and not *Anas crecca* Linnaeus, 1758.

Giant Petrel *Macronectes* sp.

A record exists of a Giant Petrel species being bought on Diego Garcia in July 1970. The specimen is now in the Ministry of Agriculture in the Seychelles and has not been identified to species level to date.

Southern Fulmar *Fulmarus glacialoides* (Smith, 1840)

A single record exists of this species being provisionally identified at sea in July 1958 at 10°S, 69°E.

Broad-billed Prion *Pachyptila vittata* (Forster, 1777)

There are records from pre-1971 and a recent claim of five Broad-billed Prions at sea at 7°S, 78°12'E on 19 February 2001. These records have been treated with caution due to the absence of substantiating evidence and the difficulty of identifying this genus at sea and also the potential vagrancy of several prion species in the Indian Ocean.

Gadfly petrels *Pterodroma* sp.

There are numerous possible sightings of this genus from BIOT waters, though no conclusive report has been published to date.

White-bellied Storm-petrel *Fregetta grallaria* (Vieillot, 1817)

There are details of possible sightings of this species in BIOT waters, though no conclusive report has been published to date.

Matsudaira's Storm-petrel *Oceanodroma matsudairae* Kuroda, 1922

There are details of possible sightings of this species in BIOT waters, though no conclusive report has been published to date.

Western Reef-egret *Egretta gularis* (Bosc, 1792)

A claim exists of a sighting on Diego Garcia in March 1996 that was attributed to either this species or dark phase Little Egret *Egretta garzetta* (Linnaeus, 1776). This record has been withdrawn.

Pelican sp. *Pelecanidae* sp.

Information of a pelican in Peros Banhos lagoon in January 2009 were passed to the author by two yachts that were there at the time, there is insufficient detail to claim a positive record.

Sparrowhawk sp. *Accipitridae* sp.

A "sparrowhawk" was seen hunting through the Downtown area of Diego Garcia on 26 December 2008; it was not identified beyond genus.

Great Snipe *Gallinago media* (Latham, 1787)

A record exists of "Eight snipe, almost certainly this species…." on Diego Garcia on 03 April 1971. As no supporting information exists and the author of the record admits uncertainty, this record has been placed in the non-verified category.

Asian Dowitcher *Limnodromus semipalmatus* (Blyth, 1848)

There is a single claim for this species in that of a lone bird on Diego Garcia on 17 March 1995. There is not enough supporting evidence to place this IUCN categorised "Near Threatened" species (with a decreasing world population of 23,000 birds) in the confirmed category.

Spotted Greenshank *Tringa guttifer* (Nordmann, 1835)

There is a claim of this species on Diego Garcia on 21 March 1995. There is not enough supporting evidence to warrant placing this IUCN categorised "globally endangered" species (with an estimated world population of 500–1,000 birds) in the confirmed sightings category.

Wandering Tattler *Heteroscelus incanus* (Gmelin, 1789)

This species appears as a captioned illustration in David Bellamy's book *Half of Paradise*, which covered the Joint Service Expeditions to BIOT in the early 1970s. It is also mentioned in an unpublished ornithological report of the 1972/73 Joint Service Expedition to the Egmont Islands, presumably the source of the *Half of Paradise* illustration. There is insufficient evidence in either of the records mentioned to differentiate this species when in non-breeding plumage from the virtually identical Grey-tailed Tattler *Heteroscelus brevipes* (Vieillot, 1816). Therefore, the records are placed in the non-verified category.

Lesser Black-backed Gull sp. *Larus fuscus* sp.

Lesser Black-backed Gull taxonomy is in a state of flux and the level of detail in the record of a single adult that over flew the accommodation area of Diego Garcia on 26 May 2005 is not sufficient to confirm identification to species level, other than saying it was a *Larus fuscus*-type.

Whiskered Tern *Chlidonias hybrida* (Pallas, 1811)

A single adult in non-breeding plumage was claimed to be seen on Diego Garcia on 21 March 1995. Non-breeding and immature plumaged *Chlidonias* terns are not so straight forward to identify. It has been proven that the marsh tern that regularly winters in BIOT is White-winged Tern *Chlidonias leucopterus* (Temminck, 1815). As there is no supporting photograph or description to substantiate the record, it is possible that the record refers to White-winged Tern and this record is therefore placed in the non-verified category.

Black Tern *Chlidonias niger* (Linnaeus, 1758)

A single claim exists of this species: a lone bird of unstated age or plumage in the Egmont Islands on 01 February 1975. Due to the lack of supporting details and the very real possibility of it being White-winged Tern, this record is treated with caution and placed in the non-verified category.

Great Skua *Catharacta skua* Brünnich, 1764

Records exist of three sightings of possible Great Skuas at sea up until 1971. As there is no supporting information or photographs and the possibility of confusion with other skuas, which may occur in the area, these records are treated with caution and placed in the non-verified category.

Pigeon sp. *Columbidae* sp.

There are unconfirmed reports in the 19th century of pigeons occurring in BIOT. Some credence is lent to these reports with the occurrence of a Rock Pigeon in 2009.

Little Swift *Apus affinis* (Gray, 1830)

An illustration captioned "Little Swift" appears in David Bellamy's book *Half of Paradise*, which detailed the activities of the Joint Services Expeditions to BIOT in the 1970's. As there are no supporting details for this bird and, because of the possible confusion with other white-rumped swifts that can occur in BIOT, this record is placed in the not conclusive category.

Pied Crow *Corvus albus* Müller, 1776
There is a single claim of this species: a lone bird on Ile du Coin, Peros Banhos on 08 October 1974. There is no supporting information and every possibility that House Crow was involved. Therefore, this record has been placed in the non-verified category.

Northern House-martin *Delichon urbicum* (Linnaeus, 1758)
Two Hirundine species were seen by the Percy Sladen Trust Expedition of 1905. Recent records suggest Barn Swallow is a likely candidate for one and it is possible that the other birds could have been this species.

Bulbul sp. *Pycnonotidae* sp.
Records exist that a bulbul species was introduced to Diego Garcia that "....became common by about 1953, but at this time it suddenly died out and was not reintroduced." It has been speculated that this species was Olivaceous Bulbul *Hypsipetes borbonicus* (J. R. Forster, 1781). If the species was ever introduced, it certainly no longer occurs in BIOT.

Golden-crested Myna *Ampeliceps coronatus* Blyth, 1842
This species was claimed to be seen on Diego Garcia in 1996. This record is incorrect and has been withdrawn.

List of non-bird species mentioned in the text with scientific names

Plants
Birds Nest Fern	*Asplenium nidus*
Neisosperma	*Neisosperma oppositifolia*
Guettarda	*Guettarda speciosa*
Cordia	*Cordia subcordata*
Lantern Tree	*Hernandia sonara*
Coconut	*Cocos nuciferus*
Fish Poison Tree	*Barringtonia asiatica*
Takamaka	*Calophyllum inophyllum*
Pisonia	*Pisonia grandis*
Scavvy	*Scaveola taccarda*
Beech Heliotrope	*Argusia (Tournefortia) argentea*

Invertebrates
Lesser Green Emperor	*Anax guttatus*
Picturewing	*Rhyothemis variegata*

Crustacea
Coconut Crab	*Birgus latro*

Reptiles and amphibians
Cane Toad	*Rhinella marina,*
Bloodsucker	*Calotes versicolor*
Blind Snake	*Ramphotyphlops braminus*
Hawksbill Turtle	*Eretmochelys imbricata*
Green Turtle	*Chelonia mydas*

Mammals
Black Rat	*Rattus rattus*
Feral Cat	*Felis catus*
Pig	*Sus domesticus*
Donkey	*Equus asinus*

References

Austin, J J, Bretagnolle, V and Pasquet, E (2004) A global molecular phylogeny of the small *Puffinus* shearwaters and implications for systematics of the Little – Audubon's Shearwater complex. *The Auk*, 121(3): 847–864.

Bailey, R (1968) The pelagic distribution of sea birds in the western Indian Ocean. *Ibis* 110: 493–519.

Baldwin, E A (ed.) (1975) A Report on the Joint Services Expedition to Danger Island in the Central Indian Ocean December 1974 to April 1975. London: MOD.

Bellamy, D J (1979) *Half of Paradise*. London: Cassell.

Benson, C W (1970) The systematic status of *Streptopelia picturata* on Diego Garcia. *Bull. Br. Orn. Club* 90: 32–35.

Bibby, C J, Burgess, N B and Hill, D A (1992) *Bird Census Techniques*. Academic Press Ltd.

BirdLife International (2004) *Important Bird Areas in Asia: Key Sites for Conservation*. BirdLife Conservation Series 13. Cambridge, U.K. BirdLife International.

BirdLife International (2008) The BirdLife checklist of the birds of the world, with conservation status and taxonomic sources. Version 1, Online http://www.birdlife.org/datazone/species/downloads/BirdLife_Checklist_Version_1.zip downloaded 11 September 2008.

Bourne, G C (1886) General observations on the fauna of Diego Garcia, Chagos group. *Proceedings of the Zoological Society London*. 1886: 331–334.

Bourne, W R P (1959) Notes on Sea Reports received in 1958–1959. *Sea Swallow*, 12: 6–17.

Bourne, W R P (1960) The Petrels of the Indian Ocean. *Sea Swallow*, 13: 9–22.

Bourne, W R P (1966) Observations on Islands in the Indian Ocean. *Sea Swallow*, 18: 40–43.

Bourne, W R P (1970) Observations of Seabirds. *Sea Swallow*, 20: 47–55.

Bourne, W R P (1971) The Birds of the Chagos Group, Indian Ocean. *Atoll Research Bulletin*, 149: 175–207.

Bourne, W R P (2001a) Observations of Seabirds. *Sea Swallow*, 50: 6–17.

Bourne, W R P (2001b) Chagos Birds. *Sea Swallow*, 50: 32.

Bourne, W R P and Nelson, J B (1976) Birds on the Chagos Bank. *Nature*, 261: 452.

Bruner, P L (1995) Avifaunal and Feral Mammal Survey of Diego Garcia, Chagos Archipelago, British Indian Ocean Territory. Diego Garcia Integrated Natural Resources Management Plan. Diego Garcia: US Department of Defence. Appendix F1.

Burger, J and Gochfeld, M (1994) Predation and effects of humans on island-nesting seabirds. In Nettleship, D N, Burger, J and Gochfeld, M (eds) *Seabirds on islands: threats, case studies, and action plans*. Cambridge, UK. BirdLife International (BirdLife Conservation Series no.1).

Burr, T A (2004) "Integrated Natural Resources Management Plan Update Diego Garcia, British Indian Ocean Territory Avifaunal Survey of 7–18 March 2008". In NAVFAC, Pacific – Naval Facilities Engineering Command, Pacific (2005) Diego Garcia Integrated Natural Resources Management Plan. Hawaii: US Department of Defence.

Carr, P (1996) Observations of the Birds on Diego Garcia 26–29 March 1996. *Sea Swallow*, 45: 95–99.

Carr, P (1997) Exercise Diego Garcia Survey Latest Update / Stop Press. *Sea Swallow*, 46: 86–87.

Carr, P (1998) Expedition Report Diego Survey 97, 4–18 August 1997 (Part One – The Seabirds). *Sea Swallow*, 47: 9–22.

Carr, P (2000) Expedition Report Diego Survey 97, 4–18 August 1997 (Part Two – The Landbirds). *Sea Swallow*, 49: 30–35.

Carr, P (2003) Further Bird Observations from Diego Garcia, 4–5 December 2002. *Sea Swallow*, 52: 21–25.

Carr, P (2004) Important Bird Areas in the British Indian Ocean Territory. Unpublished report to the RSPB.

Carr, P (2005) Diego Survey II – Expedition Report. *Sea Swallow*, 54: 6–41.

Carr, P (2006) "British Indian Ocean Territory". In Sanders, S M (ed.) *Important Bird Areas in the United Kingdom Overseas Territories*. Sandy, U.K.: RSPB. pp. 37–55

Carr, P (2008a) Diego Survey III – Expedition Report. *Sea Swallow*, 57: 16–62.

Carr, P (2008b) Royal Navy Birdwatching Society Expedition Activity. *Chagos News*, 32: 11–14.

Clement, P and Holman, D (2001) Passage Records of Amur Falcon *Falco amurensis* from SE Asia to Southern Africa including First Records from Ethiopia. *Bulletin of the British Ornithologists' Club*, Vol. 121: 222–231.

Cochrane, M C N (1992) Initial Survey of New Coral Islet off Diego Garcia Atoll. *Sea Swallow*, 41: 62.

Curtis, W F (1976) The Visit of R.F.A. Reliant to the Chagos Archipelago, 6–10 October 1974. *Sea Swallow*, 25: 11–13.

Edis, R (1998) Peak of Limuria. London: Chagos Conservation Trust.

Feare, C J (1984) Seabird status and conservation in the tropical Indian Ocean. Pp 457–471 in Croxall, J P, Evans, P G H and Schreiber, R W (eds) *Status and conservation of the world's seabirds*. Cambridge, UK: International Council for Bird Preservation (Tech. Publ. 2).

Finsch, O (1887) Ein Besuch auf Diego Garcia im Indischen Ozean. *Deutsche geographische Blätter Bremen* 1887: 30–42.

Gadow, H and Gardiner, J S (1907) The Percy Sladen Expedition Trust to the Indian Ocean. Aves, with some notes on the distribution of the land-birds of the Seychelles. *Trans. Linn. Soc. Lond. Zool.* II, 12: 103–110.

Guzman, N (2003) Wildlife on Diego Garcia. *Chagos News*, 22: 5–7.

Hillman, J C (2005) Report on the State of the Environment of Eagle Island, Chagos Archipelago. Cambridge, UK. Chagos Ecological Restoration Project, Fauna & Flora International.

Hilton, G (2002) Latest News on the Birds of the Chagos. *Chagos News*, 20: 6.

Hirons, M J (1973) Notes on the birds of Egmont – Chagos Archipelago. Unpublished report.

Hirons, M J, Bellamy, D J and Sheppard, C R C (1976) Birds on the Chagos Bank. *Nature*. 260: 387.

Howells, M J (1983) The Birds of Diego Garcia. *Sea Swallow*, 32: 42–47.

Hutson, A M (1975) Observations on the Birds of Diego Garcia, Chagos Archipelago, with Notes on other Vertebrates. *Atoll Research Bulletin*, 175: 1–26.

Lever, C (1987) *Naturalized Birds of the World*. Harlow: Longman Scientific & Technical.

Loustau-Lalanne, P (1962) The birds of the Chagos archipelago, Indian Ocean. *Ibis* 104: 67–73.

McGowan, A, Broderick, A C and Godley B J (2008) Seabird Populations of the Chagos Archipelago: an Evaluation of Important Bird Area Sites. *Oryx*, 42: 424–429.

NAVFAC, Pacific – Naval Facilities Engineering Command, Pacific (2005) Diego Garcia Integrated Natural Resources Management Plan. Hawaii: US Department of Defence.

Nyári, Á, Ryall, C and Peterson, A T (2006) Global invasive potential of the house crow *Corvus splendens* based upon ecological niche modelling. *Journal of Avian Biology*, 37: 306–311.

Pepi, V E (2005) "Avifaunal Survey Summary for Point Count Surveys Conducted July 2003 and March 2004, and Incidental Sightings of July 2003, March 2004 and January 2005, Diego Garcia, British Indian Ocean Territory". In Diego Garcia Integrated Natural Resources Management Plan. Hawaii: US Department of Defence.

Pienkowski, M W (ed.) (2005) Review of existing and potential Ramsar sites in UK Overseas Territories and Crown Dependencies. Final Report on Contract CR0294 to the UK Department of Environment, Food and Rural Affairs. London: UK Government.

Pocklington, R (1967) Observations by Personnel of R.V. ATLANTIS II on Islands in the Indian Ocean. *Sea Swallow*, 19: 38–41.

Ripley, S D (1969) Comment on the Little Green Heron of the Chagos Archipelago. *Ibis*, 111: 101–102.

Sheppard, C R C (1979) Introduction to the Joint Services Chagos Expedition 1978–79. In: Griffiths J D (ed.) *Chagos: the 1978–79 Expedition*, MOD Publication, London.

Sheppard, C R C and Seaward, M R D (eds) (1999) Ecology of the Chagos Archipelago. *Linnean Society Occasional Publications* 2.

Spalding, M (2005) The Chagos WEXAS Expedition. *Chagos News*, 26: 2–4.

Symens, P (1999) "Breeding Seabirds of the Chagos Archipelago". In: Sheppard, C R C and Seaward, M R D (eds) Ecology of the Chagos Archipelago. Otley: *Linnean Society Occasional Publications* 2. pp. 257–272

Topp, J (2003) "Editor's Note". In: Guzman, N (2003) Wildlife on Diego Garcia. *Chagos News*, 22: 5–7.

Topp, J (2006) "Editor's Note". In: Carr, P (2008) Royal Navy Birdwatching Society Expedition Activity. *Chagos News*, 32: 11–14.

Woods, J L (2002) Squadron of the Feathered Kind Visits. Tropical Times of 06 Dec 2002.

www.worldbirds.org

Useful bird guides in BIOT

The two most useful bird guides for use in BIOT are:
Rasmussen, P C and Anderton, J C (2005) *Birds of South Asia. The Ripley Guides*. Vols 1 and 2. Smithsonian Institution and Lynx Edicions, Washington, DC and Barcelona.
Skerrett, A, Bullock, I and Disley, T (2001) *Birds of Seychelles*. Helm, London

The following books have proved extremely useful for identifying vagrants:
Alström, P and Mild, K (2003) *Pipits and Wagtails of Europe, Asia and North America. Identification and Systematics*. Christopher Helm, London.
Chantler, P and Driessens, G (2000) *Swifts: A Guide to Swifts and Treeswifts of the World*. Second edition. East Sussex, Pica Press.
Feare, C and Craig, A (1998) *Starlings and Mynas*. London: Christopher Helm.
Ferguson-Lees, J, Christie, D, Burton, P, Franklin, K and Mead, D (2001) *Raptors of the World*. London: Christopher Helm.
Hancock, J & Kushlan, J (1984) *The Herons Handbook*. Croom Helm, London & Sydney.
Harrison, P (1983) *Seabirds: an identification guide* (Revised Edition). Croom Helm, Beckenham, Kent.
Madge, S and Burn, H (1988) *Wildfowl. An Identification Guide to the Ducks, Geese and Swans of the World*. London: Christopher Helm.
Marchant, J, Prater, A J and Hayman, P (1986) *Shorebirds: an identification guide to the waders of the world*. Christopher Helm.
Nelson, J B (1978) *The Sulidae: Gannets and Boobies*. Oxford: Oxford University Press.
Olsen, K M and Larsson, H (1995) *Terns of Europe and North America*. London: Christopher Helm.
Taylor, B and van Perlo, B (1998) *Rails. A Guide to the Rails, Crakes, Gallinules and Coots of the World*. Pica Press.
Turner, A (1989) *A Handbook to the Swallows and Martins of the World*. London: Christopher Helm.

Index